LSD UNDERGROUND

Operation Julie, the Microdot Gang and the Brotherhood of Eternal Love

*

David Black

2

*

***

****

BPC Publications © 2022

*

thebarbarismofpureculture.co.uk

****

***

CONTENTS

Preface

1 – The Proselytizer: David Solomon – p9

2 – The Chemist: Richard Kemp – p16

3 – The Fixer: Ronald Stark – p28

4 – Tetra-Hydro-Cannabinol – p32

5 – The Brotherhood of Eternal Love and its British Connections – p40

6 – Transatlantic Antics – p48

7 – The French Connection: Paris and Orleans – p54

8 – Ronald Stark and Ronald Laing – p61

9 – The British Microdot Gang – p64

10 – The Split in the Microdot Gang– p74

11 – Richard Kemp's Laboratory in Wales – p78

12 – Operation S.T.U.F.F. – p84

13 – Operation Julie – p89

14 – Downfall – p103

15 – Trickster – p121

16 – The Greening of Microdoctrine? – p129

EXTRA

LSD–IRA? David Solomon, James McCann and Operation Julie – p138

Bibliography – **p**163

Acknowledgements

Thanks to Harvey Mason, Andy Roberts, Catherine Hayes, Tim Scully, Dick Pountain, Stephen Bentley and the late Steve Abrams – all of whom are absolved of any responsibility for the text that follows.

Thanks to VectorStock.com for the cover background art.

Preface

Whilst on remand in Her Majesty's Prison Bristol, in 1977, Leaf Fielding, LSD distribution manager, met LSD chemist, Richard Kemp:

> Richard was a man after my own heart. We talked long and excitedly in one-hour bursts. He too had wanted to turn the world on and he'd gone a long way towards achieving his aim by producing kilos of acid, enough for tens of millions of trips...
>
> 'And look where our idealism got us.'
>
> His despondently waving arm took in the prison walls, D wing and the punishment block.
>
> 'Well we're not the first people to be persecuted for what we believe in,' I replied, 'and I don't suppose for a moment we'll be the last. We'll be exonerated in the future, don't you think?'
>
> 'Maybe. But that doesn't help us now.'
>
> The bell brought another exercise period to an end.
>
> Leaf Fielding, To Live Outside the Law

LSD Underground, the title of this book, refers to the British producers and distributors of Lysergic Acid Diethylamide (LSD) who began operating in 1968 and continued in secret for nearly a decade. The venture grew into an underground industry, supplying the festival-going youth of the 1970s with tens of millions of acid trips. The police eventually rounded up most of the gang's principals in March 1977 in what the media hailed as the 'biggest drugs raid in British history'. On 8 March 1978, at Bristol Crown Court, 29 defendants were handed down prison sentences totalling 170 years, with the sentences for the 17 principal defendants amounting to 133 years.

The first issue in writing about the defendants in the Operation Julie trial is what to call them. They have been referred to as the 'Microdot Gang', but this is a misnomer, because a split in 1973 produced two separate and independent organisations which shared a common origin. The LSD conspirators have also been called the 'Operation Julie Gang'; but that is anachronistic because it wasn't until 1976 that the police launched Operation Julie. Hence I will use the term, LSD Underground, which is more accurate and descriptive.

The present work follows several books that have appeared since the Julie trial in 1978. Three books have been written by former police officers of the Julie squad: the operational commander, Richard Lee, and undercover detectives, Martyn Pritchard and Stephen Bentley. Two books have been authored by defendants: Leaf Fielding, LSD distributor; and Christine Bott, lover of the LSD chemist, Richard Kemp. Alston 'Smiles' Hughes, another defendant, who distributed acid from his base in Llanddewi Brefi, Wales, is currently working on his memoirs in collaboration with Andy Roberts, which will be published sometime in 2022. Stewart Tendler and David May's book on the US Brotherhood of Eternal Love deals at length with that organisation's relations with their British counterparts. Lyn Ebenezer's book on Operation Julie gives the perspective of a local journalist covering the story in Wales (all these books are listed in the bibliography).

Why another book? Simply because, whatever the merits (which are many) of the above published books, some of them suffer from factual inaccuracies which can now be corrected with what historians refer to as 'updated scholarship'; and none of them present an adequate blow-by-blow account of the genesis, development and downfall of the LSD Underground in the years 1968 to 1978. Detective Inspector Richard Lee's book *Operation Julie, How the Undercover Police Team Smashed the World's Greatest Drugs Gang* attempts to make sense of the British LSD Underground as part of an international conspiracy rooted in the US Brotherhood of Eternal Love, which is described by Stewart Tendler and David May as a 'hippie mafia'. The international dimension of the LSD producers needs to be explored further and more thoroughly. Here, I attempt to unravel and demythologise it.

One of the challenges any writer presenting this history has to deal with is the age-old problem of participants offering differing accounts of the events and their interaction with each other. These accounts are often motivated by self-justification or simply the wish to tell a good story. It is necessary therefore to be sceptical on the one hand of the 'official' agenda which called to account those who broke the law and supposedly threatened public morality; and on the other hand the counter argument that the 'acid adventure' was a noble cause which just happened to be illegal – and lucrative. Corroboration – or rebuttal – has been employed whenever possible and in appropriate measure.

Operation Julie exposed a war of 'values' between the agencies of the state and its ascribed enemies in the counterculture. The LSD Underground conspirators were committed to changing mass consciousness through psychedelic enlightenment, but their 'idealism' rapidly gave way to the exigencies of running an organised crime group. Although as hippies they nominally rejected violence, one of the first things that struck the police investigators was that the organisational structures resembled the sophisticated cell-networks of terrorist groups, involving the use of aliases, secret bank accounts and safe deposit boxes, front companies, dead-letter drops, messages in code, and the like; hence the confusion that wracked the police investigation. I argue that the police, media and state had little understanding of what they were up against.

The reader of whatever opinion will find heroes and villains in this tale. The hippies were plagued by cheating, informing and paranoia; the police by corruption, bureaucratic incompetence and internal rivalry. This historical narrative investigates the motives and practices of the British LSD Underground and its American cohorts. It also shows how Operation Julie was weaponized in a culture war to suppress 'deviation' from 'traditional' values which a victorious Thatcherism came to represent in the ensuing years. Ultimately, however, it was a pyrrhic victory over the counterculture and the 'War on Drugs'.

1 – The Proselytizer: David Solomon

The 'Acid Adventure' – as Christine Bott would later call it – began innocently enough. In the last weekend of July 1968, science-graduate Nick Green hitch-hiked 200 miles from Liverpool to attend the Cambridge Folk Festival, which that year featured the Pentangle, Odetta and Roy Harper. Nick was an enthusiastic pothead, partly because his medication for epilepsy made him unable to tolerate alcohol. As was common in those days, dopers tended to find one other, and Nick, with his scouse charm, hit it off with two young American sisters, Lynne and Kim Solomon. Their father, they proudly told him, was famous in the US for his best-selling books on marijuana and LSD. Lynne and Kim invited Nick to come home with them after the gig and meet their hip parents. Nick, rapidly falling for Kim, eagerly accepted the invitation. At the Solomon home in nearby Grantchester Meadows, Nick was introduced to David and Pat Solomon. David was looking for a chemist.

*

David Solomon, born in 1925, grew up in New York. Enlisting in the army in World War II, he was excluded from combat duty after his two brothers were killed flying bombing missions over Germany. Transferred to Military Intelligence, he rose to the rank of sergeant. After his discharge in 1946, he studied English Literature at Washington Square College, New York and went on to a successful career in journalism. From 1956-1960, Solomon was an assistant editor at *Esquire* magazine. As a devotee of modern jazz, he commissioned a provocative article by Dizzy Gillespie entitled 'Jazz is too good for Americans,' which was published in the June 1957 issue. Gillespie argued: 'Jazz has never really been accepted as an art form by the people of my own country... They believe... people hear jazz through their feet, not their brains. To them, jazz is music for kids and dope addicts... Not serious music.'

Inasmuch as David Solomon could be called a 'dope addict', he took his drugs as seriously as the music. He was a habitual marijuana smoker and experimented with both psilocybin and lysergic acid diethylamide (LSD). He devoured the writings of Aldous Huxley, such as *Brave New World* and *The Doors of Perception,* and regarded him as psychedelic 'guru extraordinaire'. Solomon tried — unsuccessfully as it turned out — to get *Esquire* to publish Huxley's writings on how pharmacological innovations might facilitate a much-needed spiritual/ethical revolution.

In 1960 Solomon left *Esquire* to take over the editorship of *Metronome*, a venerable but ailing jazz magazine. According to his colleague, photographer Herb Snitzer, Solomon was hired to 'bring a more hip, Esquire-like sensibility to the magazine – more politics, culture, up-to-date issues. Solomon was hip all right... ideas spilled out of him... we were publishing a magazine that featured something truly revolutionary: our focus was on the young black jazz performers who were transforming music in America... We proselytized...'

Metronome soon acquired the reputation of being the dopers' jazz magazine in contrast to *Downbeat*, which was mainstream and 'straight'. Solomon commissioned writers of the avant-garde 'Beat Movement', including LeRoi Jones, Henry Miller, Lenny Bruce, Allen Ginsberg and William Burroughs. In Burrough's case, extracts from his novels were presented as meditations on the horrors of heroin use. But the new hipness of *Metronome* failed to reverse its decline in circulation. Solomon was sacked in summer 1961 after putting a stripper on the cover of the magazine. The magazine folded a few months later.

By this time Solomon had access to a good stash of LSD, which he kept in a safe deposit box at a Manhattan bank. As a psychedelic proselytizer he ran tripping sessions for those he thought could benefit from it, especially jazz musicians. Psychedelic aficionados have always emphasised the importance of 'set and setting' in the psychedelic experience. 'Set' is the 'mindset' of the subjective experience; 'setting' is the physical and social environment in which experience happens; as Huxley put it, 'experience is not what happens to you; it's what you do with what happens to you.' Solomon had no background in medicine or psychiatry, but he was confident enough to act as a trip-guide. Jazz clarinettist, Perry Robinson, recalled Solomon's words in preparing him for a tripping session:

> All your fears and emotions and intuitions and senses are heightened to the max. It's like complete enlightenment, it's like the first day of life. But it's going to open you up like a book, and you're going to go into your personal history. The key is not to let anything that comes up get to you. The worst thing

is to fight any of these feelings; just accept them no matter what they are.

Robinson dissolved Solomon's acid-laced sugar cube in his mouth:

> Then all of a sudden it was like the lights went on in a strange way... It opened my eyes to seeing things, like what Aldous Huxley wrote about in *The Doors of Perception*, how you start seeing minute objects and shapes. Things are alive, things are breathing, and it's the true state of being. Condensed light makes physical objects, and on trips you realise that everything is light, and you see the pure undulating energy of the universe.

Solomon took a keen interest in Dr Timothy Leary's psychedelic research project at Harvard University, and was personally acquainted with him. Leary tested psilocybin pills on student graduate volunteers, many of them divinity students. The psilocybin was supplied free of charge by the Swiss Sandoz pharmaceutical company. Then Leary met Englishman Michael Hollingshead, who had bought a gram of LSD (enough for 5,000 trips) from Sandoz. With Hollingshead's LSD, Leary entered a mode of being in which 'nothing existed except whirring vibrations and each illusory form was simply a different frequency'. It was, Leary said, 'The most shattering experience of my life... Since that time I have been acutely aware that everything I perceive, everything within and around me, is a creation of my own consciousness.' The Harvard psychedelic project immediately 'bade farewell to picturesque psilocybin'. Leary and his colleague Richard Alpert eventually conducted about 3,000 sessions for graduates and faculty members and 1,000 for outside volunteers. In April 1963, Leary and Alpert were sacked by Harvard University on the grounds that Leary had absented himself and missed his scheduled lectures, and Alpert had broken the university's prohibition on conducting drug tests with undergraduates.

Undeterred, Leary and Alpert transferred their psychedelic program to Millbrook, a mansion on a 2,000 acre estate near Poughkeepsie, New York State. This was owned by William Mellon Hitchcock, a young stockbroker on Wall Street for Lehman Brothers, and scion of the super-rich Mellon family. Hitchcock rented the main house at Millbrook to Tim Leary and his associates at a nominal rate. Leary jokingly named his enterprise the Castalia Foundation – after the spiritual sect in Herman Hesse's novel, *The Glass Bead Game*, with himself playing the part of Grandmaster Joseph Knecht. The pilgrims were prepared to pay for the psychedelic experience and turned up in increasingly large numbers. David Solomon was one of them. Solomon collaborated with Leary on an anthology for Putnam publishers entitled *LSD: The Consciousness-Expanding Drug*. The book featured Leary and various writers with backgrounds in literature, psychiatry, medicine, philosophy and theology, including: Aldous Huxley, William Burroughs, Alan Watts and Humphrey Osmond. The book was a best-seller; and Solomon was to follow it up with other anthologies, including *The Marijuana Papers* (1966), *Drugs and Sexuality* (1973) and *The Coca Leaf and Cocaine Papers* (1975).

Solomon's introduction to *LSD: The Consciousness-Expanding Drug* reads in part like a psychedelic version of a revolutionary Situationist manifesto: what Guy Debord called the 'Spectacle' Solomon called the 'Social Lie'. To the 'entrenched political establishments' psychedelics were indeed a 'dangerous subversive agent':

> By their action of swinging wide 'the doors of perception' the insights they potentiate frequently enable one to see through the myriad pretensions and deceits which make up the mythology of the Social Lie. Thus to the extent that the power structures rely on the controlled popular acceptance of the Lie to shore up and stabilize their hegemonies, psychedelic substances do indeed represent a kind of political threat. Fortunately, however, only the most static, repressive society needs worry about psychedelic subversion. Consciousness-expanding chemicals, in reality, present no threat, but rather offer hope and encouragement to a democratically oriented social structure.

In 1966, Solomon left the US and moved to Europe with his wife and two daughters. They lived in Palma, Majorca, until he was arrested and prosecuted by the Spanish police for possession of LSD. Without paying the fine, he moved on to England. In London, he attached himself to the milieu of like-minded radicals such as the psychiatrist, RD Laing, and his colleagues at the Philadelphia Association; and the researchers of SOMA (the Society for Mental Awareness, which campaigned for the decriminalization of cannabis use). In late-1967, he settled with his family in Grantchester Meadows, Cambridge.

2 – The Chemist: Richard Kemp

David Solomon, introduced to Nick Green by his daughters, was a hospitable host. As David had plenty of dope to smoke, Nick settled in and talked about his degree in oceanography from Liverpool University. David was pleased to hear that Nick had studied chemistry. In fact, he was looking for someone with chemistry training to work for him as a researcher. He believed that with the right technology and chemistry it might be possible to synthesize the active principle of marijuana, Tetra-hydro-cannabinol (THC), and put in on the market. Such an enterprise, he assured Nick, would be perfectly legal under existing English law. Nick keenly took up the job offer; knowing that the perks included his blossoming romance with Kim as well as access to David's hash.

David Solomon purchased equipment and chemicals, set up a laboratory just outside Cambridge at Waterbeach, and rented a cottage for Nick Green to live in. As Green perused the scientific research papers Solomon had collected he learned that making THC would require the precursor Olivetol, an organic compound found in certain species of lichen, otherwise known as 5-*n*-Amylresorcinol. As Nick's own knowledge of practical chemistry was limited he decided he needed expert advice. Wondering about who he could turn to, he immediately thought of Richard Kemp, a brilliant PHD student he had known at Liverpool University.

Kemp, born in 1943 to a working-class family in Northumberland, won a scholarship to Bedford School as a day-boy and went on to study science, first at St Andrews University, then at Liverpool. He graduated in 1965. By 1968 he was doing research work for a PHD on 'the nuclear magnetic resonance of fluorinated molecules'. Although Kemp and Green had never actually been friends, they knew each other from having shared a bench in a laboratory before Green transferred his studies from chemistry to oceanography. Green telephoned Kemp at the chemistry department and asked him for a favour: could he look in the university's chemical catalogues and see if there were any suppliers of olivetol listed? Kemp checked the catalogues and found there weren't any. Green was disappointed, but he suggested they meet that evening as he had something to discuss he thought Kemp might find interesting. They met at the Philharmonic Hotel on Hope Street, very near where Green was living with his parents. Green explained that he was doing scientific research work for an American business enterprise and that he had some xeroxed scientific papers which Kemp might like to look at. Also, he had some cannabis to smoke; something Kemp had never tried before but was curious about. They went to Green's house and Kemp read over the findings of the Israeli scientists Gaomi and Mechoulem, who had managed to produce THC with a synthesis of olivetol and the chemical compound verbenol. This caught Kemp's eye because he knew that that verbenol was being made by a fellow student in the university research lab. Another paper explained how to synthesize olivetol. Puffing on his first joint, Kemp told Green he was reasonably certain that olivetol could be prepared in a laboratory with the right equipment. Green told Kemp about the lab in Waterbeach and invited Kemp to come down and take a look at it. Kemp took up the invitation and hitch-hiked all the way to Cambridge. He was impressed by the expensive equipment in the lab but couldn't help noticing that it was badly organised and not very well maintained.

In the meantime, Kemp was booked to attend a chemistry conference on nuclear magnetic resonance in Coimbra, Portugal. The trip proved to be part of Kemp's political awakening. The radical students of Portugal had been inspired by the May/June Revolts of 1968 in France, but the fascist-leaning regime was intolerant of any dissent. The atmosphere in the country was tense, with troops and armoured cars on the streets. Kemp was struck by the contrast between the poverty he saw in the country and the luxurious treatment laid on by the government for the scientists at the conference, which was held under the auspices of NATO.

Shortly after Kemp returned to Liverpool he was again contacted by Green. At his next visit to the lab in Waterbeach, Kemp was introduced by Green to David Solomon. Invited back to the Solomon family home, Kemp found Solomon fascinating company and got properly stoned for the first time on David's prime hash. As Solomon listened to Kemp speaking about his chemistry studies he realised that he was meeting a major scientific talent, who was potentially very useful to him. To save Kemp the trouble of hitch-hiking back to Liverpool he gave him five pounds for the train-fare. On his next visit Kemp arrived in a car bought with some compensation money he had been awarded for injuries in a road accident.

Kemp told Solomon that the equipment at Waterbeach was inadequate for the task in hand, so it might be better if he were to try and do the syntheses at his Liverpool research lab in his spare time. Solomon agreed enthusiastically. Kemp returned to Liverpool and got to work. As this research was perfectly legal, he was quite open about it with colleagues in the chemistry department and didn't care about the raised eyebrows. Kemp came up with the goods. He sent small quantities of olivetol and verbenol to Green, who imitated the Gaomi/Mechoulem method to couple them together and produce THC. Green telephoned Kemp to say his experiment had been successful. Unfortunately, he couldn't actually prove it because he hadn't set aside a sample for Kemp to inspect and had smoked it all himself. Kemp was exasperated. It seemed that Green was more interested in getting stoned on David's hash and courting his daughter, Kim, than doing serious chemistry work.

On New Year's Eve 1968, Kemp attended a party hosted by David and Pat Solomon at Grantchester Meadows. He explained to David that making THC in any viable quantity would require a lot more investment in materials and equipment. Solomon agreed and came up with an idea for getting the project properly funded. He suggested to Kemp that he might try his hand at making lysergic acid diethylamide (LSD), which could be sold for a tidy profit and provide the needed investment money for making THC. Of course, he pointed out, making LSD would be illegal and Kemp would have to think about it very carefully.

The banning of LSD in the UK in September 1966 had been driven by a media-driven moral panic about the countercultural youth who were using it. One of the 'elders' of the counterculture was the Scottish novelist Alexander Trocchi, a former-member of the Situationist International. An incurable junkie, Trocchi had jumped bail on heroin charges in New York and fled the US via Canada. In June 1965, Trocchi organised and compèred an international poetry reading at the Albert Hall, which was attended by several thousand people. This event, billed as *Wholly Communion*, gave birth to the term, 'Underground'. In collaboration with experimental artist, Jeff Nuttall, Trocchi initiated the Art Laboratory, which put on multi-media and performance art in an old warehouse in Drury Lane.

In 1965, Timothy Leary sent Michael Hollingshead – the Englishman who had introduced him to LSD a few years earlier – on a mission to London. Hollingshead arrived with 5000 trips of LSD and a list of things to do. Firstly, Hollingshead was to rent the Albert Hall for a psychedelic jamboree with big-name rock bands and poets; with Leary himself hosting the event in his role as the High Priest of LSD. This plan never came off, because of Leary's bust for marijuana possession in the US at the end of 1965. Another part of the mission involved setting up a centre for running LSD sessions and promoting psychedelia in the arts. Hollingshead, with help from old-Etonians, Desmond O'Brien and Joey Mellen, turned a Belgravia flat into the 'World Psychedelic Centre'. For their LSD sessions, they used the book, *The Psychedelic Experience: A Manual Based on the Tibetan*

Book of the Dead, authored by Timothy Leary, Richard Alpert and Ralph Metzger. Hollingshead thought 'that London would indeed become the centre for a world psychedelic movement.' The World Psychedelic Centre soon drew in a host of media stars and musicians, including the Beatles. According to Hollingshead, the World Psychedelic Centre clientèle

> represented perhaps the seminal non-conformism of England's mid-sixties intelligentsia - not the evangelical non-conformism of such as the Millbrook sect, but an intellectualized form of psychedelic enlightenment, of which popularised Learyism was largely a culmination - that freed so many of England's educated people from the rigidity of social and class and cultural patterns which had outwardly been solidifying into right-wing Toryism. Their rebellion was typical of this period; the Establishment was the enemy...'

For several months, Hollingshead's World Psychedelic Centre team spread a lot of acid around London. The secret however, couldn't last; and it didn't. In March 1966, *London Life* magazine investigated the WPC and 'uncovered a social peril of magnitude which it believes demands immediate legislation to stop the spread of a cult which could bring mental lethargy and chaos.' A few weeks later the *Sunday People* jumped in with:

> We have obtained evidence of 'LSD parties' being held in London. We have discovered an alarming group of people who are openly and blatantly spreading the irresponsible use of this terrible drug.

> These men run what they call the Psychedelic Centre... Amongst the Centre's activities is the publication of a handbook called 'Psychedelic Manual'... a treatise on drug-induced hallucinations and other 'benefits'... These include: 'For personal power - for fun - for sensuous enjoyment.' The manual ... says the taking of LSD and similar drugs offers 'a release from our conditionings' and 'senses become more acute'. Recommending group sessions of drug-taking, the writer says 'A person should approach the experience with love and trust in the company of those he trusts.' A psychedelic experience lasts normally from eight to sixteen hours - but the results may last from several days to several months. 'The voyager should set aside at least two days for the experience itself.' This is irresponsible, dangerous gibberish.

In the meantime, while half the youth of Britain were wondering how to score their first trip on LSD, and listening to their favourite pop groups singing about it, the elders in the corridors of power were asking how soon the drug could be banned. It soon was. The media-consensus was that the drug encouraged 'moral lethargy'. One story by a tabloid hoaxer warned that LSD users were blinding themselves through staring into the sun while tripping. It was even argued that LSD could endanger national security if, for example, anarchists dosed the reservoirs (even though according to the science this would be impossible). The British Medical Association articulated the Establishment line in the *Lancet*: that LSD was essentially an anxiety-inducing drug, and therefore dangerous.

New legislation was rushed through both Houses of Parliament, and on 9 September 1966 manufacture, distribution and possession became a criminal offences, punishable by imprisonment or a fine. This, however, did little to discourage use of LSD. Indeed, in 1967 there was an explosion of LSD consumption in Britain. A good deal of the LSD was produced by Victor James Kapur, proprietor of a pharmacy in New North Road, Hackney, east London. Kapur and his distributors were not part of the emerging hippie subculture; and seem to have had no motivation beyond profit. Kapur bought his ingredients from a British chemicals company, and had them delivered to a front company he set up in West Germany. Kapur's operation, which began in September 1966, lacked the chromatographic technique necessary to chrystalize the acid. Dealers who bought the drug in its powdered form turned it into tablets or dissolved it so it could be dropped onto blotters. Kapur may have made as much as a kilo of LSD before police busted his operation in November 1967. In May 1968, Kapur was sentenced to nine years imprisonment. His chief distributor, Harry Nathan got seven years.

Like Kapur, David Solomon was motivated by the prospect of making a lot of money. But, as a disciple of Timothy Leary and as a well-known author, he was now one of the leading figures of the psychedelic 'spiritual mission'. Richard Kemp and Nick Green found his enthusiasm and commitment infectious. As Solomon could procure the necessary ingredients to make LSD from Germany, Green suggested moving the chemistry equipment from Waterbeach to Liverpool, where they would be able to set up a laboratory in his parents' house. The respectability of the household – Nick's father was a music professor; his mother the manager of an exclusive dining club for academics – would conceal the illicit goings on in the basement. Solomon thought this was a great idea. Kemp agreed to work in the new lab.

In January 1969, Kemp and Green travelled to London for a meeting with Solomon and his American business partner, Paul Arnaboldi. Arnaboldi was well-off, having been awarded a large compensation sum for a road accident in the USA. Like Solomon, Arnaboldi was a veteran of Timothy Leary's psychedelic funhouse at Millbrook. At a meeting at the Great Eastern Hotel on Liverpool Street, it was agreed that Solomon and Arnaboldi would supply the starting materials plus equipment, and Kemp and Green would produce the LSD.

Arnaboldi procured 40 grams of the starting material, ergometrine maleate, from a Mexican company in Basle, Switzerland, and sent it to Solomon in sellotaped packets hidden inside a rolled-up magazine c/o an American Express office in London. In Green's Liverpool lab Kemp used this material to make a modest quantity of LSD using the Garbrecht method of synthesis. Kemp then organised a 'sampling' of his dark syrupy acid with his girlfriend, medical student, Christine Bott, and Green. Although not of the best quality, the acid, sampled on blotting paper, was effective; all three of them tripped and became LSD devotees from that moment on. Green and Kemp passed the acid to Solomon, who in return gave them a down payment in the form of a large lump of hash. The LSD from a second production run was sent to Arnaboldi in Canada, where he was setting up North American distribution networks.

*

In early summer 1969, Solomon took his family to a villa he had rented in Majorca. Kemp, Bott and Green visited and spent weeks enjoying the sea and sun until Arnaboldi arrived from his own base on the island at Deia and suggested bluntly that it was about time Kemp and Green got back to work. There were music festivals coming up in the US, notably at Woodstock, and his distributors wanted thousands of LSD trips to sell at them. Kemp and Green returned to Liverpool, leaving Christine Bott behind to continue her holiday. In the Hope Street basement, Kemp resumed production.

According to Andy Munro, a Cambridge chemistry graduate who later joined Kemp's team, 'Many of the chemicals used are extremely dangerous, toxic and/or explosive.' The starting point for manufacture of LSD is to use ergot alkaloids to produce lysergic acid. The alkaloids are toxic and unstable; the acid is more stable, but unpredictable in its reactions with other chemicals. To make diethylamide the organic acid is reacted with diethylamine using a 'coupling agent' which binds the lysergic acid and is then displaced by the diethylamine to produce the required diethylamide. Munro writes:

> I do not propose to go into the nuts and bolts of the whole procedure. It involves ether (extremely

explosive) and huge extraction funnels, as well as the need to be done in a dark, dry environment. You can see the potential for failure, never mind death!

The other danger was contamination and overdose from the finished product. Working alone in the Hope Street basement, after his return from Majorca, Kemp successfully made the acid, but accidently spilled the flask it was in. In attempting to retrieve the spilt liquid he ingested a massive dose and experienced a trip of 'cosmic proportions'. When he recovered his faculties, Kemp returned ashen-faced to Majorca with what could be saved from the broken flask. He found Solomon and Arnaboldi squabbling over money: Solomon wanted compensation for his investments in THC; Arnaboldi wanted compensation for his trips to Mexico and Canada.

Back in Liverpool, Nick Green, working in the lab on his own, had an epileptic fit and cut himself badly. Noticeably, his behaviour was becoming increasingly irrational and aggressive. Acting on the spur of the moment, Nick eloped with Kim to get married in Scotland, which incensed David and

Solomon. Arnaboldi was of the opinion that Green was 'crazy'. The tipping point came one night in Liverpool when Nick slipped LSD into his mother's cup of tea. She collapsed, gasping in fear and clutching her throat. A doctor was called and Green confessed what he had done, pleading 'I did it because I love her. I wanted to turn her on. It's pure love that I gave her.' His parents decided not to bring charges, but banned Kemp from the house, and ordered that the laboratory in their basement be dismantled. It fell to Kemp to tactfully tell Green that it was time to wind up their project and go their separate ways.

Kemp had been neglecting his PHD studies at Liverpool University; and his supervisors were becoming restless. Although he wanted to finish his PHD, he felt he was being used just to support the theories of his supervisor, which he had little interest in. He was now tripping twice a week: 'I was far more interested in exploring the contents of my own head than in pursuing the minutiae of science to their seemingly illogical conclusions.'

3 – The Fixer: Ronald Stark

In May 1969 in Paris, a student at Cambridge University (name unknown) met 31 years old fellow American, Ronald Stark, at a left-wing demonstration. As fellow 'heads' they got round to talking about the politics of drugs. The student mentioned that he was friendly with David Solomon, who was now living in Cambridge. Having first dropped acid the previous year, Stark was very interested in Solomon's writings and said he would like to meet him in person. When the American student returned to Cambridge he told Solomon all about his meeting with Stark, who had said in all seriousness that he wanted to turn on the world to LSD. As Solomon had a similar ambition, he immediately wrote to Stark, inviting him to visit and discuss their mutual interests. In the summer of 1969, Stark arrived at Grantchester Meadows.

In their conversations, Solomon confided in Stark that he had a brilliant chemist working for him on his long-term project to produce THC. Not only that, his chemist could make LSD, for which Solomon, had access to starting materials. Stark was keen to meet the chemist, so Solomon telephoned Kemp and urged him to come to Cambridge straight away and meet someone 'really important'. When Kemp arrived, the three of them spent the weekend discussing LSD and THC production. Stark invited Solomon and Kemp to meet him in London at the Oxford and Cambridge Club on Pall Mall, where he had convinced the management that he had been to Harvard University (he hadn't) and thus qualified for membership. At the meeting, Stark proposed that Kemp come and work in his state-of-the-art Paris laboratory, which was housed at the PACS chemical company in the 13th Arrondissement.

Kemp had become aware that Solomon and Arnaboldi regarded themselves as his agents, entitled to a transfer fee plus a percentage of whatever he got from Stark. Stark was not keen on the idea of a transfer fee for someone not legally bound to his employment; and he didn't like percentage deals as they were open to double-crossing. What was finally agreed was that Kemp would work in Stark's lab in Paris on the THC project and that Solomon and Arnaboldi would be supplied with Stark's LSD at the very cheap price of 900 dollars a gram.

Just after Christmas 1969, Kemp travelled to Morocco to spend time with Stark and his British assistant, Simon Walton. For several days in Casablanca they relaxed, smoked Kif and discussed future plans. Kemp, who had been refused sabbatical leave by his university, was persuaded by Stark to abandon his PHD and sign a legal contract with him to synthesize THC, for which he would be paid living expenses and get a percentage of the royalties on sales. The three of them travelled on to Switzerland and Kemp placed the contract in a safe deposit box at a bank in Geneva. Kemp returned to Liverpool and told his supervisor of his decision to abandon his PHD.

In January 1970, Kemp reported for work in Paris, where Stark introduced him to the people he had billeted together in a roomy apartment on the Left Bank, near his laboratory. According to Christine Bott, they were 'a sexually ambiguous group of people': Stark's British boyfriend, Simon Walton;

Stark's girlfriend, Henrietta Kaimer, 'who was a prostitute with a small clientele who were high ranking members of the government'; Stark's American chemist, Tord Svenson, who had operated an LSD lab in Boston which was busted in 1967; and another American, David Linker, also gay, who had performed in the Paris production of the musical, *Hair*. Bott recalled that Linker, who was also a chemist, 'helped Richard cope with the excesses and insanities that surrounded Ron'.

Stark told Kemp he had a few hundred grams of ergotamine tartrate he wanted converted into LSD on order to complete his latest production run. Kemp expressed unease about this, as he understood that he been hired for making THC, not LSD. Stark reassured him; claiming that under French law, making LSD in bulk was legal, providing it wasn't converted into individual doses. Kemp wasn't entirely convinced by this assurance but went along with it anyhow. After another batch of LSD was produced at the lab, Kemp resumed work on the THC project, to try and crack the synthesis, using the Olivetol/Verbenol route. He managed to make a crude active amount but was still unable to produce pure, stable THC.

Stark sent Tord Svenson back to the US to organise tableting and distribution of LSD. When he got an order for a large consignment, another production run got underway in Paris using 8 kilos of ergotamine tartrate (ET). The team, Kemp included, worked at night when no one else was on the premises of the PACS chemical company. Because the purified LSD became light and dusty, there was a danger that the air could dose anyone in the building who wasn't kitted out with a mask and protective clothing.

One night Kemp put a flask containing his muddy synthesis of LSD in the freezer. Unexpectedly the contents bloomed into white crystals of almost pure LSD. Kemp had accidently discovered that the purification process could be speeded up without using chromatography. Within two weeks they produced 1,240 grams of LSD, enough for six million trips.

On visits to England, Stark had noticed that Solomon had a slack approach to security and confidentiality; talking about the 'business' to too many people. Stark advised Kemp to steer clear of him, but Kemp, according to Christine Bott, had come to see Solomon as something as a father-figure; he kept in touch with him via telephone without Stark knowing about it.

4 – Tetra-Hydro-Cannabinol

Whilst LSD research had yielded up its secrets to the counterculture, as both a psychedelic ('mind-manifesting') hallucinogen and a marketable commodity, research into Tetra-Hydro-Cannabinol (THC) was still in its infancy. But what was known about the psychedelic potential of cannabis derivatives fascinated aficionados. It seemed to some like a quest for a holy grail, not to mention a way to make a lot of money. That is why, LSD aside, Ronald Stark and David Solomon persisted in their research into THC production. One possible source of useful information was SOMA (the Society of Mental Awareness) whose director in London was the Chicagoan expatriate, Steve Abrams. SOMA had been set up in 1967 to promote a more positive attitude towards the smoking of cannabis, and to reform the punitive laws restricting it. The SOMA organisation's famous full-page advertisement in *The Times* of July 24, 1967, calling for a reform of the cannabis laws, was signed by a host of 'big names', including Nobel Prize winner Francis Crick, novelist Graham Greene, psychiatrist RD Laing, painter David Hockney, the four Beatles and various members of parliament from both sides. The statement quoted Spinoza: 'All laws which can be violated without doing anyone any harm are laughed at... will foment crime rather than lessen it.'

SOMA engaged in active research and medical programs which were affiliated to a National Health Service surgery in Notting Hill. In 1968, a parliamentary committee on cannabis chaired by Baroness Barbara Wootton considered SOMA's arguments for reform of the drug laws. During this period of official open-mindedness towards cannabis, SOMA's research wing was granted a licence by the Home Office to study THC. SOMA contacted the Israeli scientist, Mechoulam, who sent laboratory notes and a gram of olivetol in the form of a viscous oil for use as a base material. This small sample was sent for processing at pharmaceutical firm, Koch-Light. After some hitches in processing the base material, SOMA's Nobel Prize winner, Francis Crick, corrected the formula and found it worked. SOMA's chief chemist, Dick Pountain, working in a lab at the back of Chelsea football ground, converted the olivetol to Delta-8 THC, which contains psychoactive ingredients not to be found in other extractions from the cannabis plant. Then like good scientists, in Pountain's words, 'we bio-assayed it subjectively'. According to Abrams: 'It was like the very finest Moroccan kief with a hint of cocaine. It was very, very good dope and it satisfied me that all the main effects of cannabis are due to this one chemical – THC - (tetra-hydro-cannibinol).'

Abrams soon became a target of the tabloids. The *News of the World* put Abram's picture under the headline 'This Dangerous Man MUST be Stopped'. Abrams commented, 'Quite inflammatory stuff. It said he's found a legal way to make drugs. But the article had no real content... It did get round to admitting that the Home Office was aware of our experiments with THC and had no objection to them.'

In London, around mid-1969, Abrams was asked by David Solomon if he would like to meet a 'fellow American' who wanted help in obtaining scientific research information on

THC. Abrams was suspicious and reluctant to agree to the meeting, partly because he didn't entirely trust Solomon and partly because the previous two years of campaigning for SOMA had put him on his guard for a potential set-up – either by hostile Sunday newspapers, gangsters or secretive state forces. As regards the latter, Abrams had discovered that his previous research at Oxford University on Extra Sensory Perception had been covertly funded by the CIA through a front organisation called the Institute of Human Ecology (it was revealed years later that the Institute had also funded research into LSD). Abrams had become increasingly aware of Solomon's heightened profile on the periphery of SOMA and, although he appreciated Solomon's pioneering writings on LSD and cannabis, he had an instinct not to let him assume any role within the SOMA organisation. The friend Solomon wanted Abrams to meet was Ronald Hadley Stark:

> Solomon, who I'd known for a year or two, was very pushy and as soon as he learned I'd made contact with Laing or Francis Crick, or someone like that, he would be there after me. His approach was badly bungled, I became suspicious about Stark for no particular reason and at first I refused to meet him. Finally, because Solomon was being quite persistent, I reckoned I should let this guy Stark know that I had nothing of use to him. I had instructions for making small quantities of THC, a gram or two at a time. But that assumed you had the starting material to begin with, so that couldn't be

of any interest. I said he could meet with Adam Parker-Rhodes, our pharmacologist and Dick Pountain, our chemist, if he gave a hundred dollars donation to SOMA. The cheque bounced but cleared the second time... When Stark met them he gave them his business card, for a company called Interbiochemical Ltd. The company had an office in Ghana.

Dick Pountain denies that he ever met Ronald Stark. Pountain adds:

> Shortly after the successful synthesis I quit, on the very mundane grounds that Steve wouldn't pay me what he had promised. The whole affair was a matter of some press interest at the time, and the New Statesman's gossip column came out with a preposterous story that SOMA's chief chemist had left after a dispute because he was a Freudian while Abrams was a Jungian! It's true that I'm a Freudian, but one who likes to get paid... Something also missing is that Abrams sold my lab book, in which I had written up the synthesis in proper Imperial College style, to David Solomon. It was found when Operation Julie arrested him, and two officers came to visit me just before the trial and interrogated me about my possible involvement, which I denied and they accepted.

If Pountain's lab book was sold to Solomon, then it may well have found its way to Stark, possibly for a good price. In any case, Abrams didn't trust Stark and saw him as something of threat. Abrams asked Glynne Webley-Everard, of Avalon Botanicals, SOMA's pharmaceutical company, to check Interbiochemical out through his company accountant's office in Accra, Ghana. They discovered that Stark owned almost a controlling interest in the State pharmaceutical house there and had a contract to supply the Ghanaian government with pharmaceuticals. Abrams decided at this point to telephone Bing Spear, head of the Home Office drugs inspectorate:

> I said, 'This guy is heavy duty, I've not come into contact with anyone like him. He's not a drug dealer; he's Mafia or CIA or both, but it's the heavy mob.' I'd never made a call like that to anybody but I wanted to cover myself and I felt I should give him this information.

The following year, 1970, Stark, accompanied by David Solomon, turned up at Abrams' new place-of-residence, Hilton Hall, near Cambridge. This classically landscaped property had been the well-known haunt of the Bloomsbury Group; and busts of Virginia Woolf and Lytton Strachey stood in the hall. An old Bloomsbury survivor, the writer Bunny Garnett, had given over use of the house for a cheap rent to a group of writers and artists, including Jenny Fabian, author of the best-selling paperback novel, *Groupie*; and Johnny Byrne, Liverpool poet and *Doctor Who* screenwriter. Solomon introduced his friend as 'Mr Simpson' but eventually Abrams, who knew Solomon had been talking about Stark for months, asked him: 'Are you the legendary Ronald Stark?' 'Mr Simpson' denied this at first but later owned up, identifying himself as 'Ronald Hadley St. John Whitney Stark'.

Stark moved into Hilton Hall for a few months and with the offer of financial support tried to persuade Abrams to resurrect SOMA, which by this time was foundering due to the backlash against the 'cannabis lobby'. Stark became a sort of resident millionaire. Content to sleep on the couch rather than in a posh hotel, he would happily take a dozen people out to dinner at the local Monsieur Andre's restaurant and would pay the Hilton Hall electricity and telephone bills. Before Stark's arrival, Solomon was visiting Hilton Hall regularly, and as the residents knew he was dealing acid they became slightly paranoid about possible police interest in the place. They noticed, for example, a car frequently parked with its lights on nearby, which would cruise past them as they walked home late at night. The appearance of Stark coincided with the lifting of the apparent surveillance. Abrams recalled:

> We were quite aware what was going on with the Brotherhood in case someone would turn up with a suitcase full of acid. We didn't go so far as to take part in any of Stark's activities. We just benefited from his largesse.

Stark told Abrams he had studied at John Hopkins University, and worked as biochemist at Cornell University. But Abrams' unease about Stark was growing:

> He had a card that said he was a director of ICI! I couldn't help overhearing his phone calls

because I had a little device on the [stereo] amplifier, a little suction coil that was basically a telephone amplifier; it didn't do a very good job of amplifying your voice but you could have a three-way conversation with it. I discovered by accident that if I had that turned on and somebody was having a conversation I could listen in on it. I mean you didn't listen compulsively to Stark's conversations; they were generally unintelligible. I became concerned because he seemed to be involved with arms trading, there were indications of terrorist connections. This is pretty vague, but he seemed to be buying and selling chemicals which often by their nature, and with the quantities he was dealing with, seemed to have nothing to do with making drugs or drug factories.

Later Stark, whilst tripping, told Abrams his game plan for THC. Stark explained that he wanted to make THC dimethylheptyl derivative. He had worked out eight of the fourteen stages of synthesis with a 90 per cent yield in each stage and wanted to make it by the kilo. He estimated that the production cost would be £4,000 a kilo (£30,000 in today's money); but this was much too expensive for a commercial product. Stark thought it would be cheaper to extract it from the natural cannabis product rather than THC synthesis, but he reckoned he needed £800,000 to set up a production laboratory for this purpose. He wanted to raise half a million dollars himself to get the project going and get someone else to front it for him. Stark said that the dimethylheptyl synthetic THC derivative had been made up at ETH Zürich (Swiss Federal Institute of Technology) for the Hofmann-Laroche pharmaceutical company. He had taken 250 µg of it and been heavily overdosed for 3 days. Abrams said 'I've heard many people challenge these premises about the immense power of dimethylheptyl and Stark is the only person I spoke to who claimed to have taken it.'

In his quest for a process of extracting the THC dimethylheptyl derivative from the natural cannabis plant Stark visited Afghanistan at least once in the early 1970s, at a time when the brothers Aman and Nasrullah Tokhi were supplying the US Brotherhood of Eternal Love with large shipments of hash. Stark wanted the Tokhis to run a hash-oil facility he was trying to set up; and wanted the Brotherhood to put up half a million dollars to develop his dream project of turning Afghan cannabis into a hallucinogenic THC concoction which could be turned into crystals. Stark was also working on a minister in the Afghan government to set up a penicillin factory as a front.

5 – The Brotherhood of Eternal Love and its British Connections

From the early 1950s onwards the CIA experimented with LSD on thousands of people, mostly without their consent, in order to weaponise it for chemical and psychological warfare. By the early 1960s the CIA experimentation program, MK-Ultra, had determined that LSD was of less use to them than had originally been hoped. But by this time LSD had begun to escape the clutches of the agency and its assets in the medical and scientific professions. By the end of the 1950s, thousands of patients had been treated with LSD therapy for mental illnesses and addictions to heroin and alcohol; and hundreds of scientific papers on the potential therapeutic effects of LSD and other hallucinogens had been published by researchers and practitioners. In reaction to these dissenting opinions on LSD, the official line was laid down in 1959 at a Macy Foundation conference, chaired by Dr. Paul Hoch, CIA consultant and US Army Chemical Corps contractor. Hoch dismissed claims about LSD's therapeutic qualities. LSD and mescaline were, he pronounced, 'essentially anxiety producing'. The official line was, however, increasingly ignored; and the federal legislation to properly enforce it hadn't yet been enacted.

During the early 1960s, Michael Druce, a London commodities dealer, bought LSD from the Swiss Sandoz pharmaceutical company and sold it on to customers in the USA. As an established broker and trader, Druce made his profits by storing merchandise against price rises. As a specialist in chemicals trading, he was able to approach producers directly. But in 1962, under pressure from the US government, Sandoz restricted exports and Druce had to look for an alternative supplier. He found one when, in 1963, the Sandoz patent on LSD expired, and the Czechoslovakian state pharmaceutical firm, Chemapol, began to produce it. Chemapol's trading wing, Exico, marketed LSD in 1 milligram vials for small orders or in 100-milligram ampoules of powder for bulk purchases. Exico's business in London was handled by Ronald Craze, another Englishman. Craze began exporting a Czechoslovakian LSD to customers in the United States, including Timothy Leary and friends at Bill Hitchcock's Millbrook estate in Poughkeepsie. Druce and Craze got together and became business partners.

After LSD was made illegal in both Britain and the United States in 1966, Druce and Craze stopped trading in it. However, their prime American customers wondered, would they be prepared to procure and export raw materials and specialist lab equipment for LSD production in the USA, if the end-users were beyond British jurisdiction?

*

One American chemist who needed the chemicals was Tim Scully, who served his LSD-making apprenticeship with Owsley 'Bear' Stanley. When Owsley started making LSD in 1964 it had been in the form of a green goo which, though effective, wasn't pure enough to crystallize. He solved this problem by mastering chromatography – a technique for separating out a mixture of chemicals. To produce a standard dose of 300 µg (micrograms) he used triturate boards to produce uniform tablet sizes, dispersing the LSD content evenly in tribasic calcium phosphate.

In late-1965 advertisements began to appear in California posing the question, 'Can you pass the acid test?' Properly defined, the 'Acid Tests' were events organized by the Merry Pranksters, a group of Californian pagans led by Ken Kesey, author of *One Flew Over the Cuckoo's Nest*; featuring music played by the Grateful Dead; with LSD supplied by Owsley. In early 1966, Owsley was taken on by the Grateful Dead as their sound engineer. Owsley had experience of engineering for radio and television, but he didn't have enough knowledge of electronic circuit design to implement his ideas for customised equipment. Tim Scully had the technical know-how; and he also wanted to make LSD with Owsley. Scully had studied math and physics at the University of California and was employed by Atomic Laboratories Inc. as an electronics design consultant. Owsley offered Scully and his friend Don Douglas a chance to travel with him and the Grateful Dead to Los Angeles and do electronics and roadie work for the band. By the end of July 1966, Owsley had sold his LSD product and decided to set up another lab, with Scully and Douglas as assistants. This meant leaving the band, as he had earlier agreed that he would not work in a lab while traveling or living with them.

In autumn 1967, Tim Scully and Don Douglas were supplied with chemicals and equipment by Owsley for a production run of LSD at a secret lab in Denver, Colorado. The lab, which produced several hundred grams of LSD, was never discovered by the authorities and was dismantled as soon as the run was completed.

In 1967 the California State Senate made simple possession of LSD a misdemeanor offence, and manufacture and supply were made felony offences, punishable by one to five years in prison. Owsley wanted to get the LSD from the Denver lab tableted distributed so he could retire from the business unscathed. But by this time the media were covering (and denouncing) the 'freaks' of the new hippie movement in San Francisco; and Owsley had achieved unwanted fame as the 'Acid King'. His 300,000 doses of White Lightning acid fed the multitudes who attended the 'Human Be-In' event at San Francisco in January 1967. His purple-coloured LSD tabs were consumed at the Monterey rock festival in June that year. One of the performers, Jimi Hendrix, celebrated his own trip with the song, 'Purple Haze.' Owsley's legend would later be celebrated in the Steely Dan song, 'Kid Charlemagne'. Owsley, however, was still in legal jeopardy. In December 1967, his tableting facility in Los Angeles was raided by agents of the Bureau of Drug Abuse Control, later renamed the Drug Enforcement Agency (eventually, after much legal wrangling, in 1970 Owsley went to prison for two years). In October 1967, he told Scully, who was looking to establish another LSD lab, 'You're on your own.' Scully remained in the game. He was loaned some money by Bill Hitchcock, and made his first purchases of ergotamine tartrate from Druce and Craze in January 1968.

In February 1968, Scully opened a second Denver lab. In the LSD purification process, Scully was able to demonstrate a phenomenon known as 'piezoluminescence', which had been worked out by Owsley on a smaller scale. In piezoluminescence, LSD crystals are so pure that they give off flashes of light when shaken, stirred or crushed. Scully found a new collaborator in Nick Sand, a young chemist from New York, who had moved to Cloverdale in California. Having been introduced to Sand by Owsley, Scully came to an arrangement with him to have his acid tableted.

In the spring of 1968, Scully made about 20 grams of LSD, enough for 100,000 trips. Unfortunately, while Scully was away from his lab on a visit to San Francisco, the local police were alerted to a bad corpse-like smell coming from the house. They broke in and traced the smell to spilt chemicals in the basement. The next day, police scientists identified traces of LSD. When Scully's lab assistants, Rory Condon and Ruth Pakhula, returned, unaware of the raid, they were arrested.

Tim Scully learned of the bust and avoided arrest, though he knew that documents in the house might well incriminate him. He had lost his lab equipment and his two assistants, but he still had a good supply of the raw materials he and Nick Sand had bought from Druce and Craze in London; and some chemicals from Sand's front company, D&H Custom Research. Sand agreed to finance a new lab for making LSD in return for Scully teaching him the process he had learned from Owsley.

Nick Sand, like Bear Stanley, had previously used the Hell's Angels motorcycle gang as distributors of LSD and STP (2,5-Dimethoxy-4-methylamphetamine). Scully, however, regarded the Hell's Angels as unscrupulous, violent and dangerous. Scully was acquainted with another network of dope smugglers whom he respected for their integrity and philosophy of non-violence: the Brotherhood of Eternal Love.

The Brotherhood of Eternal Love had built up bases – as utopian-inspired communities – in California, Oregon, and Hawaii. Being idealists didn't stop them from becoming one of the most successful drug-smuggling operations in the world. Although Owsley Stanley had a low opinion of the Brotherhood, his apprentice, Tim Scully, having met John Griggs at Billy Hitchcock's house in Sausalito, had been very impressed by him. To Scully, the Brotherhood of Eternal Love (at least in their determination to disseminate LSD as a social good) had a philosophy which was genuinely spiritual and non-violent. In the summer of 1968, John Griggs and Michael Randall of the Brotherhood visited Hitchcock in Sausalito. The Brotherhood, says Scully, 'were having trouble getting as much as they wanted to distribute, so when I came and said, "I'd like you to distribute the LSD I make," they were very happy'. Tim Scully's collaboration with Nick Sand and the Brotherhood led in November 1968 to the establishment of another underground LSD lab in Windsor, near Santa Rosa, California.

In his new partnership with Sand, Scully insisted that they sell everything they made at their new Windsor lab through the

Brotherhood and drop production of STP. According to Scully, 'Owsley Stanley talked me into making some STP. I don't feel good about having done that; STP turned out not to be a good psychedelic.' He adds that STP 'lacked heart. It did not lead to experiences of oneness the way that LSD often did. And quite a few people had terrifying experiences until they learned how to correctly use the drug'. Scully's priorities were to buy more raw materials and make money to pay the legal fees of his two assistants who had been busted in the Denver lab (the charges were eventually dropped because the police search had been carried out without a warrant).

*

Michael Druce and Ronald Craze had already ready supplied Scully and Sand with ingredients for LSD manufacture when, in June 1968, they took a plane to California. The two Englishmen stayed with Bill Hitchcock at his house in Sausalito. In his memoirs Craze claims he wanted investment money to establish a firm to provide livestock feeds for developing countries by means of new production methods. Craze says he genuinely believed that the new business – called 'Alban Feeds' – would be legally above board and not just a front company. Druce, however, had convinced him that supplying the materials Sand and Scully wanted would provide the economic basis for developing the livestock feeds business. Nick Sand met the two Englishmen at the airport in San Francisco and showed them the 'scene'. Michael Druce, for all his front as a straight businessman, was familiar with the ways of the Millbrook fraternity; he even occasionally indulged in psychedelic drugs himself. In contrast, Ronald Craze, by his own account, was a 'straight' who found the behaviour of the psychedelic fraternity bizarre.

Nick Sand did the negotiating with Druce and Craze during their visit. Sand, having made a lot of money from making STP provided the money, and Hitchcock acted as his nominee. A third of the money Druce and Craze received from Sand was for investment in Alban Feeds – in the form of a convertible debenture – while the other two thirds was a down payment on a shipment of ergotamine tartrate and lysergic acid.

*

Scully recalls of Owsley Bear Stanley:

> When I was working with Bear, he and I took an acid trip with Richard Alpert one day in 1967 where we were planning the strategy of turning on the world, modest as we were, and one of the things we agreed on was that if we just turned on the United States it would be like unilateral disarmament. We really had to make sure that every country in the world got turned on, particularly those behind the Iron Curtain, or else it would be a very bad thing geopolitically. And so we talked to the Brotherhood and they made an effort to spread it around the world. And they did get our LSD into Vietnam and behind the Iron Curtain and all over.

His ultimate ambition was still to make 200 kilos of acid – enough for several hundred million good doses – and give it away to help change consciousness on a global scale. As he says now, 'That latter fantasy did not happen.' Nick Sand recalled of himself:

> I was considered as some sort of mad man psychedelic commando because I'd go anywhere, do anything... If we could turn on everyone in the world then maybe we'd have a new world of peace and love. We had the insane desire to risk our freedom and be what we thought were American patriots.

47

On 4 August 1969, the Brotherhood community was shattered by the sudden death of John Griggs from a drug overdose at their commune on their secluded ranch at Idyllwild in the San Jacinto Mountains. After Griggs' death Michael Randall took over the Brotherhood's LSD distribution system and married Griggs' widow, Carol.

6 – Transatlantic Antics

Ronald Stark's arrival in California in 1970 connected the Brotherhood of Eternal Love and their chemists; the British chemical suppliers Druce and Craze; and (at arms length) Richard Kemp in Paris and David Solomon in London. In Lee and Shlain's book *Acid Dreams*, the account of Ronald Stark's first meeting with the Brotherhood of Eternal Love goes as follows.

In August 1969, Ronald Stark drove across San Jacinto Mountains of California and descended on the bungalow and teepees at the Brotherhood of Eternal Love's Idyllwild ranch with an offer they couldn't refuse. Stark was carrying a bottle containing a kilo of pure LSD which he told the hippies had been made at his laboratory somewhere in Europe. Stark talked about his expertise in scams: smuggling drugs in consignments of Japanese equipment, utilising business fronts in West Africa, and moving money through a maze of shell companies set up by his lawyers in various continents. However, he explained, he also had a mission: to use LSD in order to facilitate the overthrow of the political systems of both the capitalist West and communist East by inducing altered states of consciousness in millions of people. Stark also hinted that he was well-connected in the world of covert politics.

The account is largely true in spirit but what actually happened was that in spring 1970 (not summer 1969) Stark's envoy, Tord Svenson, arranged a meeting for him with Tim Scully and Nick Sand. Tim Scully initially met Stark and shortly afterwards took him to meet Nick Sand at his ranch in Cloverdale, California. Scully recalls:

> [Ron Stark] brought that LSD along as his calling card. By the way, it wasn't in a bottle, it was in a plastic bag. Nick remembered it as being a pound while I remembered it as being a kilo. He claimed to have European laboratories that could produce an unlimited amount of LSD and all he lacked was American distribution. I was thrilled to hear that because by then some of the gumption had leaked out of my enthusiasm for saving the world by making LSD. I still believed that it would be a positive force but I was becoming less and less convinced that simply spreading LSD to the four winds would save the world while at the same time I was free on appeal bond from the bust of my second Denver lab and facing a possible total of 56 years in Colorado state prison. Over a period of days Ron managed to convince us to introduce him to the Brotherhood and we took him down to the Brotherhood Ranch in Southern California.

Stark entered the world of Brotherhood's LSD subsystem at a time when the British commodities dealers, Michael Druce and Ronald Craze, seemed reluctant to deliver the raw materials they had been paid for in advance. When the flow of materials from England to the US dried up, Nick Sand, accompanied by his smuggler colleague, Donald Munson, flew to England to see Druce. They were offered excuses about various difficulties and delays. But the most important excuse Druce kept to himself: he had been visited by a detective sergeant from Scotland Yard, who informed him that raw materials in an illegal LSD lab in the US had been traced back to his company (the US lab, raided in Denver in June 1968, had been Scully's). The officer warned Druce that if he wanted to stay out of trouble with the law he had better not supply any more chemicals that might be used for making LSD.

As far as Sand was concerned, Druce and Craze had been paid to obtain lysergic acid and ergotamine tartrate. But now they weren't coming up with the goods, and showed no inclination to pay back the money that had been advanced to them. For a solution Ronald Stark had a devilish trick up his sleeve. In a safe deposit box in Hamburg was a stockpile of nine kilos of ergotamine tartrate Craze had stored there. The stockpile was a strategic asset of Alban Feeds: its market value was likely to increase over time; and it was collateral for loans from the bank. To facilitate the scam Stark used Lester Friedman, a chemistry professor who served as a consultant for Nick Sand. Friedman approached Craze as the representative of a firm called Inland Alkaloids, in order to make a bulk purchase of ergotamine tartrate. Craze sent documents for the sale, expecting payment in return, but heard nothing. Craze thought he had ensured that the chemicals could not be collected without proper authorization, but his instructions had not been specific enough. Stark's assistant, Simon Walton, walked into the firm's offices, presented documents for the order, and walked out with the nine kilos of ergotamine tartrate. Inland

Alkaloids was in fact nothing more than a front company with a Swiss postal box number. The directors were listed as Lester Friedman, and Simon Walton. Craze was convinced that Druce, who had been swindling money from their company, had been complicit in the scam, so he ousted him from the business. But Craze also wrote letters to Sand, Friedman and Hitchcock, telling them that the scam had ruined his business and he wasn't prepared to let the matter drop. Craze was soon visited in London by Nick Sand and Lester Friedman. According to Craze,

> Nick said that he was sorry for me but that there was nothing he could do to help me. Perhaps I should put it down to bad judgement and bad company and forget the whole thing as he couldn't see how I was going to get anywhere. I told him that wasn't an option. I had lost everything and my only way of surviving was to track down who was behind Inland Alkaloids, and if I couldn't do it myself I would have to go to the police...

Next, Craze got an invite from a 'Professor Ronald Stark' to meet him at the Army and Navy Club, a plush gentleman's club on Pall Mall, at 3 o'clock the following afternoon. When Craze arrived, Stark shook his hand, motioned him to two chairs in the far corner of the room, and ordered coffee and biscuits. Stark said that he had been asked to meet Craze by 'some friends' who had been disturbed by letters Craze had written to them:

He asked me politely if I could explain what happened. So I told him the whole story of Inland Alkaloids, Mike Druce's treachery, the destruction of our business and possible bankruptcy. He listened patiently and when I finished he shook his head saying it was a most distressing business. He said that he wasn't without influence and with my permission perhaps he could talk to the bank.

Then, Craze recalls, Stark came to the point:

> He still needed supplies, we no longer delivered. In my heart I knew that I would never catch up with the people behind Inland Alkaloids, and it might be dangerous involving the police – I just wanted to survive, and be shot of the whole mess. Stark was very polite and pleasant. I finished my coffee, and with assurances that he would do everything he could with the information given to help us, I took my leave. He had read me correctly. I was to learn five years later that he had been sent over to see if I should be eliminated, and to arrange for a contract on me, but he had reported back that I was small fry, and as long as the organisation took preventative measures, I would probably cause them no more trouble.

Craze's claim that he later learned he was being assessed for 'elimination' contract must be treated with scepticism, as there is no record of anyone in the Brotherhood of Eternal Love or its LSD sub-system ever carrying out retribution by assassination (which is not to suggest that crossing Stark was risk-free: according to an FBI report in 1962: 'Stark is reported to possess a sidearm and his mental condition is reported to be questionable. Therefore care should be exercised in contacts with him').

Craze resented his erstwhile partner Druce for ripping off their company's money, but his own self-image as a 'legit' entrepreneur, blissfully unaware of any illegality, never convinced Nick Sand; or Tim Scully, who says,

> Craze was very disingenuous in claiming that all of that money was intended as an investment in Alban Feeds. The amount that was invested in Alban Feeds was essentially a tip or a bribe for Druce and Craze... I believe that Druce and Craze already knew that they were going to have trouble selling us more ergot alkaloids at the time when they accepted a large order from Nick.

Nick Sand later said he saw none of the ergotamine tartrate consignment he had helped to extort from Craze; although Stark had assured the Brotherhood it was safely stashed in Tangiers. Tim Scully says, 'Ron Stark and Nick Sand competed for the Brotherhood of Eternal Love's favors and Ron Stark eventually won.'

7 – The French Connection – Paris and Orleans

Ronald Stark was always careful to compartmentalise his activities; only telling his colleagues about them on a 'need to know' basis. It is therefore unlikely that Richard Kemp was in on, or even knew about, the scam Stark and his contacts in the Brotherhood of Eternal Love had perpetrated on the Englishmen, Michael Druce and Ronald Craze. In the early months of 1970, Kemp was hard at work in Stark's Paris laboratory. In May 1970, Stark and Kemp took the LSD from their production run in Paris to Zurich for delivery to Stark's smuggling contacts in the Brotherhood of Eternal Love. Kemp didn't get to meet the smugglers but, at the Grand Hotel Dolder, Stark did introduce him to two of the Brotherhood's American chemists, Lester Friedman and Nick Sand. Sand gave Kemp a packet of powdered psilocybin as a gift. Stark kept this meeting of minds brief; Kemp wasn't told anything about the two Americans' connections to the Brotherhood of Eternal Love. Sand returned to the US after making some banking arrangements with Stark. Friedman had been on a visit to Israel, where he had been consulting the scientists Gaomi and Mechoulem on THC. Friedman promised to visit Stark's lab in Paris to advise Kemp on the THC research.

In Zurich, Stark collected chemicals from his safe deposit box and loaded them into the boot of a Ferrari GT 250 he had just bought. En route back to Paris, he and Kemp had a run-in with French customs, who demanded that duties be paid on the chemicals. Customs officers were also interested in the packet of powder Kemp had in his possession, which was the psilocybin Nick Sand had given him. But after satisfying themselves that it wasn't cocaine or heroin, they didn't investigate further.

In August 1970, Stark suddenly decided to move production from Paris to Orleans. He set up a lab in the outhouses of a medicine firm and rented a residence for the crew in nearby Cléry-Saint-André. Stark insisted that the move was necessary because he had received a warning that the Paris lab was in danger of being raided at the behest of the US Drug Enforcement Agency (DEA). According to Martin Lee and Bruce Shlain in *Acid Dreams*:

> While pursuing his exploits as an LSD chemist, he [Stark] communicated on a regular basis with American embassy personnel, and on numerous occasions he hinted at ties with the intelligence community. At one point he told an associate that he shut down his laboratory in France on a tip from the CIA.

When British police inspector Richard Lee later investigated Stark's movements, an informant he called 'Nancy' told him that she 'strongly suspected Stark was involved with the CIA and had friends in the American Embassy'. Whatever the truth of these suspicions, the tip-off came via the Brotherhood. Lee writes:

56

Nancy went on to say that something happened towards the end of 1970, details of which she did not know, but it resulted in one of the major Brotherhood figures visiting Stark and Kemp in France and telling them to close things down and cool it.

Tim Scully thinks the warning came from Stark's Brotherhood contacts. Scully had been driving a truck loaded with tableting equipment when he spotted clear signs of surveillance and had to abandon it. He says: 'I think that the extreme heat around that machine caused him to close the Paris lab and move to Orleans.'

Lester Friedman visited the Orleans laboratory to discuss the THC research and evaluate the equipment. He suggested buying a vapour phase chromatograph and an infra-red spectrophotometer. Kemp was sent to London to buy the equipment from the Gallencamp company. Kemp made the purchases, picked up Christine Bott in his Range Rover, and took her off to Paris for a few days. They disembarked from the Harwich ferry at Le Havre and drove towards the Belgium-France border. When Bott tried to turn on the heater, she found it didn't work because a bottle containing some clear liquid had been stuffed into the ventilator tube. She threw the bottle out of the car as they approached the border and were stopped by French customs. The customs officers weren't convinced that the equipment in the boot was for non-commercial use and accused Kemp of trying to evade payment of duties. Kemp and Bott were taken to an office to be interrogated just as Bott realised she had ingested LSD from the bottle. Bott managed to present herself as ill rather than tripped-out and they were allowed to proceed the next day. When Bott returned to the UK she took up a post at Nobles Hospital on the Isle of Man.

Stark, ever security conscious, was annoyed with Kemp over the incident; and even more so after Kemp and Walton took the Ferrari on a trip across the channel. When British customs at Dover demanded an import duty for the brand new Swiss-registered car, Walton argued that as a non-resident British citizen he was entitled to import it without having to pay the duty. Customs officers then ran a police check on Walton and discovered he had two convictions for heroin possession. Kemp and Walton were body-searched and the car was thoroughly examined. The custom officers neglected, however, to look inside Walton's briefcase. If they had they would have found documents relating to a purchase of several kilos of ergotamine tartrate. Kemp, greatly annoyed with Walton, went on to visit Christine Bott in Liverpool. When he returned to Paris he incurred Stark's wrath for not checking the customs requirements. Kemp, however, felt that if there had been a security lapse it was Stark sending him across a border with someone convicted for heroin possession. Stark also objected to Christine Bott's visits but, as Stark and Linker entertained visitors themselves, Kemp resented the double standard.

As David Linker was spending less time at the lab, Kemp was left doing most of the work. Although he was now able to isolate THC, the product decomposed immediately, so he couldn't produce a stable batch. Stark was paying Kemp's living expenses and keeping him supplied with hash, but Kemp wanted his working relation formalised regarding salary, tax etc; and Stark seemed to be in no hurry to sort it out. When Stark decided on another huge production run of LSD, Kemp decided to quit; not because he didn't want to make LSD, but because he didn't want to work under anyone, especially Stark. Kemp recalled:

> I said that I was willing but I felt that I should be paid well for doing it, which I certainly had not been up to that time. The truth of my employment with Ron Stark is that when I left I had less money than when I went there. Ron and I had several pretty bad rows over the next few weeks. I felt that his security was very bad, and that lots of people knew about me, who I was and what I was doing, but I was completely in the dark about what was happening...
> I decided to quit.

Solomon and Arnaboldi, on hearing of Kemp's decision, came to Paris to see him and suggested that he return to England and work with them to set up their own lab. Stark gave Kemp severance pay in the form of 200 grams of LSD. David Solomon wanted 240 grams of LSD as a pay-off for recruiting Kemp less 20 percent of it to be paid to Arnaboldi for supplying ergotamine tartrate. Solomon put his case during a meeting at Stark's favourite Chinese restaurant in Soho, London. Stark at first exploded in anger, but then agreed.

In 1971, Kemp had enough equipment and materials supplied by Solomon and Arnaboldi for a 'mobile lab'. His initial modus operandi was to rent a property somewhere in London, set up the lab, do a production run, then move to another house. When Kemp and Bott moved to a flat in Westbourne Grove Terrace in London, Stark visited and noticed a flask of LSD crystal in the freezer. He commented, prophetically as it turned out, 'Of course you know it's not a good idea to have a lab in the place you are living.' Bott concurred. Kemp had seriously considered doing a production run there in the flat, but there was a danger the neighbours might notice the constant noise from the pump. Kemp loaded his gear into a Bedford van and stored it in a lock-up in Bristol. He travelled the country picking up various pieces of equipment and found a suitable location for a lab on a run-down housing estate in Liverpool.

Meanwhile Stark moved out of Orleans and set up a new lab in La Clocheton, Belgium which was tucked away in the premises of Louvain-le-Neuve University. It seemed like a perfect cover: university staff thought Stark was a genuine scientist; and that the lab was making legitimate chemicals for export to Switzerland. Leading Brotherhood of Eternal Love organiser, Michael Randall, travelled to La Clocheton under an assumed name and stayed in the town with his family. Randall's order for LSD was shipped to New York concealed in a Jaguar car belonging to Stark.

Stark made no secret of his dislike of Solomon and Arnaboldi, and no doubt tried to dissuade Kemp from working with them. Stark and Kemp continued to meet socially throughout 1971, including at the Glastonbury Festival, which was well supplied with their acid. In December 1971, Stark made one last attempt to get Kemp to come and work with him now he had moved out of Orleans and set up a new lab in Belgium. Kemp turned down the offer and never saw Stark again.

8 – Ronald Stark and Ronald Laing

Stark, like Solomon, Kemp and Bott, was interested in the ideas of psychiatrist Ronald D Laing, whose work with colleagues of the Philadelphia Association had involved experimental treatment with LSD. Laing argued that people are socially conditioned to regard the external experience of space and time as 'normal and healthy'. The space explorer had become the modern hero; but for Laing it made far more sense to 'explore the inner space of time and consciousness' as a 'desperately urgently required project for our time'. Timothy Leary, who met Laing in the US in 1964, said: 'Ronnie Laing and I had much in common. His books on behaviour change harmonised with my work on interpersonal behaviour.' Leary, however, was 'dismayed' by Laing's belief that insanity was a creative resolution of emotional conflicts. In Leary's view human evolution depended, 'on finding and training the intelligent ones who will guide the species forward'.

In January 1970 an Orange County judge handed Leary a ludicrous sentence totalling 20 years for two minor marijuana offences. As Leary's friends organised a defence campaign, the Brotherhood of Eternal Love paid the Weather Underground $25,000 to free him; a task made much easier by his transfer from Fulsom Prison to the minimum security establishment at San Luis Obispo. In September 1970, Leary, according to his own account, took his life in his hands and climbed along forty yards of telephone cable which ran twenty feet-high from the prison roof to a telegraph pole on the outside. With fake passports, Leary and his wife, Rosemary, slipped out of America in disguise and flew to Algeria to stay with members of the Black Panther Party, who had been provided with an 'embassy' by the Algerian government. Leary was still a fugitive when Ronald Stark approached Laing in late-1970. Steve Abrams recalled:

> The Stark business culminated when I arranged for him to be analysed by Ronnie Laing. It was at Stark's request. He was interested in what Laing would do with him and also what he could get out of Laing. So at a certain point Stark insisted on taking acid with Ronnie and Utta Laing. I think Utta took a small dose of 150 to 200 mics, Stark took a large dose of 300 or 500 and insisted that Laing take a huge dose, though actually even a large dose of acid just tends to start off the process. The three of them have this trip, and at the top of the trip Stark makes his pitch. I heard this from all three participants – from Ronnie, Utta and from Stark – they all told the same story: Stark said that Leary was on the run. Leary's story was over and Leary wasn't the right chap; they wanted Laing to take over, not as hired help but as Boss. All the pharmaceutical companies, all the protected investments would come under his control. If he agreed he was now worth fifty million dollars and everybody worked for him, including Stark – that's the way Stark

put it. Then to cap it off Stark said, "Look, respectfully Ronnie, what are your orders?" And Ronnie said to Stark, "Get the fuck out of my house!" He threw him bodily into the street as he was well known to do to people sometimes. Stark got into a taxi and went round to Glynne Webley-Everard's house where he met me. I remember him getting out of a taxi and saying "Ronnie's fucked my head". All I could tell was that he'd had acid with Ronnie, he was very, very stoned and didn't know what he was saying or doing'.

Stark had taken Laing on in a tripping contest and lost.

9 – The British Microdot Gang

David Solomon had a network of trusted associates for distributing Richard Kemp's LSD. One of them was George Andrews, who was working with Solomon on the anthology, *Drugs and Sexuality*, published in 1973. Andrews in turn recruited the writer, Alexander Trocchi, to find bulk buyers. Paul Bennerson, who used the foolishly chosen alias, 'Robert Greenwood-High' ('Bob High' for short) was Solomon's chief courier. Solomon's largest shipments went to the Israeli, Izchak 'Zahi' Sheni, who had addresses in London and Amsterdam, and an international network of his own distributors.

Solomon, using the alias, 'Dr Andressen' established a front company named Inter-Dominion Associates to obtain ergotamine tartrate. Solomon collected the material from the West German company, Rentschler, in Laupheim and delivered it to Kemp. The deliveries took place in Zurich, where Kemp stashed the material in a safe deposit box until it was needed for LSD production in the UK. Once Kemp converted the materials into LSD he took a consignment to Geneva and put it in a safe-deposit box to be collected by Paul Bennerson.

Bennerson rented a flat as a distribution centre at Graveley. Kemp had misgivings about him because had been a recent mental patient and seemed at times to be 'rather unstable'. Solomon didn't seem overly concerned about this and insisted that Bennerson just needed a bit of 'support'. Kemp regarded Solomon's general approach to practical matters as rather slap-dash. Although Solomon had bought some wooden tableting boards to put the LSD into capsules at the Gravely base, he seemed content just to market it as 'blotter acid'. Solomon moved from Grantchester to a house in Fullbrooke Rd, Cambridge, but when Kemp turned up there he was dismayed to find Solomon hosting a large coterie of admiring hippies and being as usual over-talkative. Kemp noticed that Solomon took a dangerous delight in taking people into his confidence.

Solomon introduced Kemp to Henry Barclay Todd, a former accountant who had served two years in prison for theft and fraud. Since his release in 1968 Todd had travelled to many countries, enjoying his hobby of mountain-climbing, and financing his travels by means unknown. Now working as a porter at a Cambridge hospital, he was also dealing in LSD, and reportedly gave Francis Crick, the Nobel Prize-winning discoverer of DNA, his first acid trip. In the spring of 1971, Todd was given the job of marketing manager for Kemp's LSD.

Solomon moved his distribution operation from Bennerson's flat in Gravely to a house in Fletching, East Sussex. Yet again Kemp was disturbed to find Solomon's daughters and friends turning up there. As Solomon had decided to make the Fletching house his family home, Kemp decided to keep his distance from Solomon by renting a flat with Bennerson in Bristol and not telling Solomon the address.

Solomon showed Kemp where their LSD and money was stashed by the Roman Road near the Gog Magog Hills in Cambridgeshire. This seemed to be secure, but Kemp soon discovered that Bennerson had been dipping the cash stash. Kemp alerted Henry Todd, who suggested that Bennerson be immediately dropped from the team. Bennerson, when confronted by Kemp, confessed to taking the money, claiming he had just borrowed it. To gently unload him, Kemp paid him off with a £2,000 handshake.

Henry Todd, who found it expedient to avoid Solomon as much as possible, recruited Reading University dropout Brian Cuthbertson. He was a good find, as he had been importing LSD in liquid form from the US and knew how to make it into tablets. Cuthbertson in turn recruited Leaf Fielding, a dope-smuggling anarchist he had known at Reading University, to tablet the LSD for Todd's distribution network. Fielding recalls:

> In the 60s I was an 'acid freak' – one of a group centred around Reading University whose lives had been transformed by the powerful psychedelic. Acid had, we thought, given us a collective vision of a saner, safer future, one where human interactions would not be based on fear, greed and coercion.. Unlike many similar groups throughout the country, we did not confine ourselves to talking. In 1970, together with a bunch of similarly-minded people from Cambridge, we began to manufacture and distribute small quantities of LSD. Our conspiracy was on its way.

At his interview for the tableting job Todd asked Fielding, 'What do you think about acid?' Fielding replied: 'Acid isn't susceptible to easy analysis. Let's see... LSD is probably the best hope the human race has got of coming to grips with its problems.' Todd responded, 'Fair enough. I think pretty much the same myself.' Todd then proceeded to explain the security arrangements befitting the 'very high stakes' they were playing for. The arrangements were certainly those befitting of a secret underground organisation. Shopping bags containing thousands of newly minted tablets were exchanged for bags containing pure crystal acid for the next tableting run in such genteel settings as the teashop next to the entrance to Kew Gardens ('amazing cakes and scones'): 'If one of us doesn't make it we default to a fall-back option four hours later.' A phone call arranging a meeting for a chat at the pub at five on Saturday meant meet at the pre-arranged rendezvous at three on Thursday. The only organisation to be spoken of was Todd's business front, Intertrans. Hippie dress was ruled out; only business suits and short haircuts were in order.

Another Intertrans recruit, known as 'Chip' was assigned to work with Fielding on tableting. Together they rented a flat in Fulham to live in and a bedsit in Oxford Street for the tableting operation. Their first run produced 40,000 micro-cubes from ten grams of crystal. Several other runs followed. Security required that they didn't stay in any one place for too long. They moved from Fulham to Twickenham, and moved the tableting operation from Oxford Street to Richmond.

Tableting LSD was dangerous work, requiring masks and rubber gloves to protect against contamination. One day Chip was contaminated through sleeping on a pillow that had absorbed LSD from his hair. He had a very bad trip, vowed never to take drugs again, and quit. Weeks later it was Fielding's turn to overdose. In his book he describes what happened after he absorbed a massive dose of LSD which got into a cut in his hand through a tear in a rubber glove:

> The floor was a mass of writhing tendrils. I sank down into it, unable to move for over four million years. Generations grew up, grew old, died and were reborn on the little rock spinning around a fire in space. Through the confetti of millennia I grew tired of the interminable human story, but it rolled inexorably on and on, cruelty upon kindness upon cruelty, until mercifully at the smoking end of time, Lord Shiva danced the world out of existence.

*

Henry Todd and David Solomon weren't getting on. To Todd, Solomon was careless and a security risk. To Solomon, Todd was greedy and untrustworthy. Kemp, Solomon and Todd met in St James Park for a business meeting, which developed into a heated argument about money. Both Todd and Kemp were worried about Solomon's poor security practices such as, in this instance, shouting about their problems in a public place. The new arrangement with Solomon was 'don't call us, we'll call you'.

According to Kemp, 'Solomon was obsessed with the idea that people were trying to screw him out of his share of the money.' Solomon figured that if he could run an LSD business himself, he would be free from what he thought were the excessive claims on the profits exercised by Kemp, Todd, Cuthbertson and Arnaboldi. Solomon had bought enough equipment and ergotamine tartrate to set up his own LSD production venture. All he needed was a chemist. He turned to Dick Pountain, SOMA chemist and writer for *Friends* magazine. Solomon drove up to Scotland in his new 3.8 Mark 2 Jaguar and rented a holiday chalet in Pitlochry, Perthshire in which he planned to set up a lab. When Kemp got to see a photograph of the house, he warned Solomon that as a wooden structure it would be too much of a fire risk to use as a laboratory. In any case, Pountain dropped out; in correspondence with me he confirmed: 'I was indeed approached by Solomon to work for Julie, but I declined his kind offer once I recognised him as a foul-tempered sociopath...'

With the Scottish venture aborted, Solomon was left holding a kilo of ergotamine tartrate. He took this round to Kemp's London home and offered it to him for £3,000. As Kemp had just made 250 grams of LSD at his lab in Liverpool he fancied a break, but Solomon was persuasive and Kemp agreed to buy it. In the early summer 1972, Kemp bought another 2 kilos of ergotamine tartrate from Solomon.

Solomon, now living at Randolph Ave, Maida Vale, London, introduced Kemp to Gerald Thomas, another veteran of Leary's retreat at Millbrook. Thomas, a chemical engineer from Baton Rouge, had moved to England and started his own chemical equipment business. Solomon knew him as a smuggler of large consignments of hash from India to New York. Together, Solomon and Thomas concocted a plan to make synthetic cocaine. Thomas had been working on it but his chemistry skills weren't quite up to the task. Solomon recruited one of his

Cambridge contacts, Andy Munro, as chemistry consultant. Munro, now studying for a chemistry MA at the University of East Anglia, was reluctant to do illegal practical lab work himself, so Solomon turned to Richard Kemp. To make the proposition of cooking synthetic cocaine more appealing Solomon had rented premises for a lab very close to Kemp's home in Westbourne Park. This was too close for comfort as far as Kemp was concerned. He snorted some of Thomas' synthetic cocaine but wasn't impressed and turned down the assignment.

Solomon and Thomas' shelved their plan to produce synthetic cocaine. Thomas was inducted into the Microdot Gang on Solomon's recommendation and given the job of tableting the acid in Kemp's Westbourne Park flat. According to Leaf Fielding, Thomas was entrusted with a sizeable bottle of LSD crystal which he was supposed to put into tablets but, 'When Richard got it back it had mysteriously shrunk. Light-fingered Gerry played no further part in the nascent acid ring.' In Kemp's account, he paid Thomas £400 to tablet a gram of LSD, then unloaded him when he didn't do the job yet still demanded more money. David Solomon was more forgiving of Thomas and carried on working with him on 'other' projects.

In autumn 1972, David Solomon visited his old acquaintance Timothy Leary in Berne, Switzerland. Leary had been arrested and imprisoned by the Swiss authorities at the request of the American DEA, who wanted to extradite him. Leary was 'befriended' by Michel Hauchard, an arms dealer who had been forced into exile by the French government. In return for protection from the law and hospitality at a luxury house he owned, Hauchard demanded that Leary hand over the publication rights of his forthcoming book, *Aim for Life: Confessions of a Hope Fiend*. Leary had little choice in agreeing to these terms, but told Hauchard that his friend, the Englishman Brian Barritt was the co-author. Between Leary and Barritt it was agreed that Barritt would pass on the royalties to Leary but would gain the kudos of being Leary's co-author, even though the whole book was written by Leary. David Solomon, who had considerable experience in the publishing world, had a hand in the negotiations with Bantam Books for a $250,000 deal. He also took with him a good supply of acid from Kemp's lab on his visit.

In the spring of 1973, Richard Kemp and Christine Bott took a trip to India. They had an address for a house in Almora, Uttarakhand, which David and Pat Solomon had rented some months earlier. But when Kemp and Bott turned up at the house they learned that the Solomons had travelled on to Nepal. Kemp and Bott were taken in by a Danish hippie woman who was in charge of the house. Bott found it idyllic and had no desire to leave; whereas Kemp was restless and wanted to carry on the search for the Solomons. Bott later reflected:

> I felt I could spend a lot of time on that hilltop without missing any of the comforts of the western lifestyle. And yet I allowed Richard's will to override my own. I thought I would be able to come back. I didn't see that I was choosing to turn away from a chance that life had offered me and I had not learned that chances are to be seized, they do not

remain open indefinitely. It was one of the many nodal points in my life where alternate paths were clearly open... And so once more I followed my man.

Kemp and Bott took a plane to Kathmandu, Nepal, which to Bott seemed like being propelled back into the 'Middle Ages'. They still couldn't find the Solomons so after a few weeks exploring they took a plane back to London. David and Pat, they discovered, had returned from their trip and were back at their apartment in Maida Vale. Unluckily, Bott had contracted hepatitis in Nepal and had to spend three weeks in hospital. David Solomon had rented a villa in the south of France and invited Kemp and Bott to spend the summer there. Bott relaxed and recovered from her illness. Kemp and Solomon discussed how they were going to get their next supply of ergotamine tartrate.

When the summer ended they packed into Kemp's Ranger and headed for Switzerland. In Zurich, David and Pat rented a car and crossed into Germany to collect the ergotamine tartrate. Christine Bott went to a bank to collect the money to pay for it from a safety deposit box. The plan had been to store the tartrate in a deposit box Solomon had rented in another bank. But Solomon's lack of planning put the whole operation at risk. Kemp had expected the three kilos of ergotamine tartrate to be packed in six sealed flat plastic bags of a half kilo each for easy storage. Solomon instead returned from Germany with a load of boxes containing 60 glass bottles. Asked by a flustered Kemp 'How are we going to stash this lot?' Solomon replied they could just empty the contents into one plastic bag. Kemp exploded:

73

You have no fucking idea how poisonous this stuff is! It has to be handled very carefully. We can't hurry things and risk inhaling it. No, it's too dangerous, we'll just have to find a way to stash the bottles for now and work out how to move it later.

The bottles, when packed into boxes, wouldn't fit into Solomon's safe deposit box. Solomon told the bank supervisor that the boxes contained 'rare books', which seemed unlikely as the bottles could be heard clinking. For security, the packages were removed from the bank the next day and buried in the woods. Kemp had them dug up nine months later and taken to England.

10 – The Split in the Microdot Gang

A dispute developed within the Microdot Gang regarding the strength of their LSD tablets. Albert Hoffman's original Sandoz product had contained 250 μgs (micrograms) per tab. However, Owsley, in the US, had upped the dose to 300 μgs per tab. According to Christine Bott, Owsley's standard was followed by Richard Kemp, who was convinced that 300 μgs was required for a proper psychedelic experience. In Leaf Fielding's account, however, Kemp argued for 250 μgs, whereas Cuthbertson and Todd thought 200 μgs was sufficient. In any case, when Kemp bought some of his own LSD at a festival the effects seemed to him a bit under par, so he asked Andy Munro to test it with an ultra violet spectrophotometer at his university lab. When Munro found that each tab contained only 150 μgs at most Kemp was outraged. Unlike Todd, with his taste for high living, Kemp and Bott rejected material affluence and looked forward to a self-sufficient 'good life' of goat-breeding and organic farming. To them, making money out of acid may have been necessary, but it was a necessary evil. The diluting of the trips was a betrayal of the 'mission'. Kemp confronted Todd, who promised to investigate and make sure it didn't happen again. Kemp however, insisted that from now on he himself should take charge of the tableting. As Todd wouldn't agree to this, Kemp decided it was time to part company. However, according to author Andy Roberts who spoke to someone close to both Todd and Kemp, the tipping point was Kemp's discovery that Todd had invested heavily in General Franco's Spanish Highway Project. Solomon, for his part, was glad to see the back of Todd, and told Kemp that he had always known Todd would screw him over.

*

In documents from police files on the political views of members of the group, Richard Kemp is described as, 'right-wing until midway through studies at Liverpool; converted to left-wing revolutionary'. Dr. Christine Bott is noted as having attended RD Laing's seminars on radical psychiatry in London. She is described as left-wing, as are Mark Tcharney (like Bott, an NHS doctor), Andrew Munro (Cambridge chemist), Martin Annable (former Reading University student radical) and Alston Hughes (professional dope-smuggler). The political views of Henry Todd and Paul Arnaboldi are listed as 'unknown'. Brian Cuthbertson, Todd's assistant, is described in police files as 'slightly right of centre'. David Solomon was thought to have been a member of the Communist Party of the United States, although when the Operation Julie police later investigated him they were told by the FBI that this could not be verified. They did learn, however, that Solomon had served with US Military Intelligence during the Second World War. In the police files the 'motivations' are described as 'financial' for all the suspects, except Kemp and Bott: 'Motive for suspected LSD activity: a catalyst for British revolution by youth brought on by the use of LSD.'

One thing the police files showed no indication of was that the British Microdot Gang had split into two completely independent enterprises with their own laboratories and distribution networks. Richard Kemp's operation now consisted of himself as chief chemist; Christine Bott as his assistant; and David Solomon and Paul Arnaboldi, who both handled distribution as well as supply of chemicals and other materials. In breaking contact with Henry Todd and Brian Cuthbertson, Kemp lost his tableters and the extensive network of distributors Todd had recruited in Reading and Cambridge. Todd and Cuthbertson had lost their brilliant chemist but they had no intention of giving up on the LSD business. Todd bought and stockpiled 15 kilos of ergotamine tartrate plus equipment from West Germany and elsewhere, having covered his tracks with a host of aliases. For the chemistry Todd turned to Andy Munro, who was now an MA student at Essex University. Previously, Munro had been reluctant to serve as anything more than a 'consultant' but with Solomon now out of the way he was persuadable; Todd recruited him as the group's chief chemist. Cuthbertson served as distributor and tableter. Todd, Munro and Cuthbertson established 'mobile' lab facilities at Cambridge, then Chesterfield in Derbyshire, but soon decided that a more permanent site was needed. They set up a laboratory at 23 Seymour Road, a large detached house in the south London suburb of Hampton Wick, which Todd bought under an alias for £33,000.

After the split in the Microdot Gang, Leaf Fielding concentrated on running his health food shop in Reading. In any case after his accidental overdose, he couldn't face tableting again. When Todd got production up-and-running again, he brought Fielding back in as chief distributor, with the assurance that he wouldn't have to do any more tableting. Fielding recruited as his sub-distributor Russell Spenceley, who had moved to Maisycrugiau, Dyfed. Spenceley supplied Alston Hughes in Llanddewi Brefi, Ceredigion, who in turn supplied John Preece in Birmingham, Douglas Flannagan and Tony Dalton in London, and William Lochhead and John McDonnell in Wiltshire. Todd employed Martin Annable to collect the money for previous deliveries at pre-arranged drops or meeting places. Fielding searched the south of England for an accessible hiding place in the woods for stashes of money and acid. He chose Caesar's Camp, a wood near Bracknell in Berkshire. The stash-points were identified by scratch marks on nearby trees. Boxes containing hundreds of thousands of acid tablets were buried in one spot; stashes of sales money were buried in another hole dug three hundred yards away. Richard Burden, owner of the Last Resort restaurant in London, handled exports via Izchak 'Zahi' Sheni, an Israeli who had addresses in London and Amsterdam.

11 – Richard Kemp's Laboratory in Wales

By the end of 1973 David Solomon had procured nine kilos of ergotamine tartrate for Kemp, which was stashed in a Swiss safe-deposit box. To convert it to LSD Kemp needed a well equipped laboratory in a secluded spot, safe from prying eyes. Paul Arnaboldi put up the money for the new lab. Arnaboldi was now quite flush, having converted his income from LSD into bonds with a high interest yield. In June 1974, Arnaboldi bought a mansion called *Plas Llysin* in Carno, Mid-Wales to house the lab. Arnaboldi moved into Plas Llysin with the cover story that he had bought the mansion as a retirement home for his mother in Florida; and was writing a biography of John F Kennedy. As Kemp knew that Arnaboldi and Solomon didn't get on he didn't tell either of them about the other's involvement.

About 50 miles from Plas Llysin, Kemp and Bott bought a secluded cottage to live in called Penlleinau, near Tregaron in Ceredigion. The purchase was helped with loans from Mark Tcharney and his partner Hilary Rees, who lived eight miles away in Esgarwein, Uchaf. Both of them, like Bott, worked as NHS doctors. Kemp and Bott's cottage had two acres of land to support living the good life of self-sustainability. Bott, a keen supporter of organic farming, and member of the Soil Association, bred goats. Their furniture was sparse, they didn't install central heating, didn't have a television set or eschewed consumer luxuries. The water for their large vegetable garden came from a well which they dug on a spot pointed to by the local diviner.

In autumn 1974, Kemp met up with Solomon on a visit to London. Solomon and his smuggling partner, James Johnstone, had imported some hash oil from India on sheets of blotting paper. Johnstone was a painter, and the blotting paper, wrapped in thin plastic, had been concealed under a thick layer of paint on his canvasses. Solomon wanted Kemp to extract the oil from the sheets of blotting paper but Kemp wasn't interested. Without Kemp's help, Solomon and Johnstone managed to extract the oil from the blotting paper with carbon tetrachloride. As there was a risk that the strong smell of the chemicals would arouse the suspicions of the neighbours, Johnstone stashed the oil behind a dustbin in Clifton Road. It was a bad choice, because the dustbin belonged to a residence for police officers, one of whom challenged Johnstone as a suspected burglar. A fight ensued and Johnstone was arrested. He told the police that as he had dysentery from a trip to India he had rushed in their back yard to relieve himself. He had £300 in cash on him which he claimed was from the sale of a painting. That he was in the business of selling paintings could be verified by another buyer he was on his way to see. This turned out to be Solomon, who confirmed his story. Johnstone, charged with assault and released on bail, absconded and was never seen again.

There was another problem created by Solomon's choice of collaborators, which must have chilled Kemp to the bone. In June 1973, Solomon's associate Gerald Thomas had been arrested in Canada when customs officers seized seven kilos of hash he had imported from India. Thomas had been renting a warehouse in London to stash documents and equipment related to drugs manufacture. As the address of the warehouse was on a business card he was carrying when arrested, Thomas assumed the Canadian police would ask their British counterparts to carry out a search. Released on bail, Thomas telephoned Solomon from Canada and urged him to remove compromising materials from the warehouse. Solomon, however, took no chances; he collected the contents and dumped or destroyed all of them. When Thomas next telephoned Solomon he was enraged by Solomon's ruthlessness. Solomon's response was that under the circumstances Thomas shouldn't be contacting him and told him not to call again. Thomas then wrote an angry racist letter to his girlfriend in London, Shirley Burridge, saying 'I'm going to show the dirty jew bastard and the rest of his grotty crew.' Shirley showed the letter to Solomon, who destroyed it but told Kemp about it. Solomon said he knew so much about Thomas' criminal career that he didn't think Thomas would rat on him. But they couldn't be sure that he hadn't. Kemp, appalled by Solomon's judgment in choosing his associates, advised him to get out of the country for a while. In early 1975 Solomon took another trip to India and Nepal.

In April 1975, Kemp moved his LSD-making equipment from the Bristol lock-up to the cellar of the Plas Llysin mansion in Carno. Once the lab was set up, a big production run was imminent; then disaster struck. One morning, as the rain was clearing, Richard Kemp was driving his Range Rover between Tregaron and Carno, with Christine Bott in the passenger seat, and the Grateful Dead blaring on the stereo. The back of the vehicle was loaded with sacks of stone slabs which had not been properly secured. On a sharp bend in the road, the load slid to one side, causing the car to veer across the wet tarmac. Kemp lost control and crashed into an oncoming car. Kemp and Bott were unhurt, but in the vehicle they hit the Reverend Eurwyn Hughes was badly injured and his heavily-pregnant wife, Sheila, suffered fatal injuries. Kemp's vehicle was impounded by the police and he was charged with causing death by dangerous driving. Kemp was 'shattered' by the incident (evidently, he was not on acid at the time) and the LSD enterprise was put on hold. Arnaboldi returned to Majorca. When Solomon returned from his eastern travels Kemp went to see him in London and told him he was being prosecuted for a motoring offence (he didn't mention the fatal nature of accident). Solomon reported on his own problems with the police. The London Met had raided his house, asking him about LSD, but hadn't found anything incriminating. Perhaps it was due to Solomon's dealings with Timothy Leary on his book deal in 1972. Or was it because Thomas had grassed? Who knew?

Kemp was convicted of causing death by dangerous driving, fined £100 and banned from driving for 12 months. He resumed production of LSD in March 1976. For the chemicals, equipment and housing Kemp and Arnaboldi had, between them, invested about £60,000. Christine Bott served as Kemp's chauffeur, ferrying him to and from the lab, where he worked for up to 48 hours a shift. Arnaboldi kept watch, spending a lot of time doing work on the roof of the building, from where he could check the surrounding land for intruders.

Kemp now had the expertise to break down the tartrate and convert the residue into high quality LSD crystals in less than a month. By May, production was completed. Kemp's had converted seven-and-a-half kilos of ergotamine tartrate into 1,800 grams of LSD, which was enough to make nine million microdots. Kemp and Arnaboldi dismantled the lab and destroyed the equipment, throwing some of it down the well of the mansion.

Arnaboldi departed, taking his share of LSD crystals – 450 grams – back to Majorca. Arnaboldi had wanted his acid tableted before delivery, but Kemp refused as he had so much tableting to do himself. This caused a falling out, but months later Arnaboldi sent Kemp a friendly letter offering to buy Kemp's bonds for £20,000.

On Kemp's next trip to see Solomon in London, Solomon complained of being broke, having lost his investment in Nepalese oil when he was busted bringing it into India and fined heavily. Kemp gave him the good news that he had produced a lot of LSD he wanted distributed. They agreed on a 50-50 split of profits between the two of them.

Solomon planned to do another book, this time with Kemp's friend, Mark Tcharney. This served as cover for Tcharney's role as a courier. Tcharney delivered Kemp's microdots via a dead letter drop at Calmsden, in the Cotswolds, where Solomon rented a weekend retreat. Solomon passed on a good portion of the acid for international distribution to Izchak 'Zahi' Sheni, who had addresses in London and Amsterdam, and was being supplied by Todd's group as well. All was going smoothly, or so it seemed. Signs of surveillance such as, for example, strangers in the distance, apparently working as surveyors, were balanced against the need to get too paranoid. In any case, if the police were really onto them, surely they wouldn't have allowed the production and distribution to take place as it did. Surely?

12 – Operation S.T.U.F.F.

By 1973 the US authorities had successfully broken the Brotherhood of Eternal Love's LSD and cannabis sub-systems. Leading members of the group were now in prison, on bail awaiting trial, or on the run. Agents of the American Drugs Enforcement Agency and the Belgian police raided Ronald Stark's laboratory at La Clocheton, only to find that he had disappeared, along with his Brotherhood associate, Michael Randall. Meanwhile the British police hadn't quite cottoned onto what was now an LSD conspiracy in the UK. Police intelligence files from 1973 referred to a 'Microdot Gang' operating in Britain, but offered barely a clue as to who they were.

In November 1974, Detective Inspector Richard Lee, then head of the Thames Valley Drug Squad, was running Operation STUFF – 'Stop Unlawful Free Festivals.' Most of the free festivals were held in Wales and the south of England in places such as Windsor, Watchfield, Stonehenge and the Meigan Fayre in the Preseli Mountains. The 1974 Free People's Festival in Windsor was broken up by a force of 800 police officers, who arrested 500 festival-goers. Lyn Ebenezer, author of *Operation Julie*, calls the free festivals 'probably the closest manifestations of the mind revolution that LSD proponents campaigned for.'

For the first half of the seventies, Lee's team of cops-pretending-to-be-hippies attended the Windsor and Reading festivals every year and in one instance infiltrated an undercover officer onto the festival organising committee. From their reports, it was clear that LSD was very much in demand and that there was a lot of it about; so much in fact that Lee couldn't accept the view of the Home Office and Customs - based on annual seizures of 20,000 tabs nationwide - that 'the use of LSD in Britain was restricted to a small number of people'.

Lee approached the Central Drugs Intelligence Unit (CDIU), a non-operational body newly set up in 1973 at Scotland Yard to collate information on the British drug scene and store it on a computerised database. When CDIU 'denied having any information which showed LSD to be a problem', Lee thought, 'To be told flatly that there was nothing did not make sense.' Later in 1975, Home Office drugs inspector, Bing Spear, told him that as early as 1971 his department had reported large shipments of ergotamine tartrate to the USA by Druce and Craze's company, Alban Feeds. Spear also found that a large number of LSD microdots, seized across the world, 'originated from one common source which, in all probability, was somewhere in Britain'.

Lee discovered that an investigation as far back as 1971 had been getting near to the truth but suddenly collapsed when the gang Thames Valley Police Drug Squad and HM Customs were watching was robbed of money and drugs by officers of the London Metropolitan Police. According to Thames Valley Detective Constable Martyn Pritchard, the 1971 investigation did, however, reveal enough to register suspicions 'that a big LSD factory was in business', run by the shadowy 'Microdot Gang'. Lee was told by a drug-dealing informant he calls 'Swan' that in one instance in 1971, Met officers were paid £3,000 to grant bail for a major LSD distributor so he could flee to the Netherlands. Files Lee obtained from HM Customs' special investigators corroborated this claim. According to Lee, 'The customs files also suggested that substantial corrupt payments had been made to London police officers for protection by the LSD distributors. This made the necessity for secrecy even more important.' All this pointed to the likelihood that the CDIU had tried to cover up the corruption in the Metropolitan Police Drugs Squad. Lee was now discovering how embarrassing his own enquiries were becoming, and not just for the Met; for he was given the vague but forceful warning from on high, 'that he was not to do anything that might embarrass Her Majesty's Government'.

For corrupt officers of the London Met, as described by Pritchard, cannabis dealers, unlike acid-heads, were the low-hanging fruit. In the early 1970s, with cannabis imported and distributed by various networks, there were inevitable conflicts – sometimes violent – between rival gangs: rip-offs, turf wars, suspicions of informing, etc., all of which could be exploited by the police. Cannabis stolen by bent officers in faked-up arrests was sold on to their criminal associates or informers. Busting acid-dealers was harder work. Acid shipments were small in bulk so could be easily hidden and transported without fear of sniffer dogs. Also, in the event of a bust, tiny LSD tabs could be flushed down the drain in an instant.

In 1975, Martyn Pritchard, working undercover for the Thames Valley Drugs Squad, infiltrated a gang of dealers in Reading. As a result, three of them were arrested in possession of several kilos of cannabis and a thousand LSD microdots. One of them, John Redfearn, was released on bail in the hope that police could follow him to his supplier. Redfearn was traced to a hippie commune near Tregaron. This was the first hint of a Welsh connection, and it was strengthened when a dealer arrested in Australia with 1500 microdots turned and named his supplier as Richard Burden, who owned a restaurant in London called the Last Resort. The microdots had come from 'somewhere in Wales'. This information was sent on to London. In police interviews with Redfearn and people arrested for possession of LSD, the name, 'Smiles' and the place, Llanddewi Brefi, kept coming up. 'Smiles' turned out to be Alston Hughes. According to police files, Hughes was dealing acid in the early 1970s with Russell Spenceley, who had since moved from Reading to Maesycrugiau, Dyfed.

Inspector Lee, who in 1975, had only the faintest idea of what he was up against, prematurely organised a raid on Hughes' home at Y Glyn, Llanddewi Brefi, on 16 April 1975. His decision was based on information from the local police drug squad that renovations on Hughes house indicated he had constructed a sophisticated stash-point. The raid ended in fiasco after Lee telephoned the village police station to pass on a message to one PC Lake. The constable's wife took the call, and was told by Lee that he would be seeing her husband at the Y Glyn address. Mrs Lake rushed round to Y Glyn and asked Hughes to tell PC Lake to contact her when he arrived. Hughes, hardly believing his luck, removed his stash to a hiding place in a nearby quarry and presented a 'clean' house when the raiding party eventually arrived.

13 – Operation Julie

Despite the setbacks – or because of them – a police conference was held in Swindon on 12 February 1976 to discuss a strategy to tackle LSD production and distribution in the UK. It was attended by representatives of five provincial police forces plus Scotland Yard and the Central Dugs Intelligence Unit. Richard Lee proposed assembling Britain's first nationwide, multi-force special squad. The Metropolitan Police, who knew about the botched raid Lee had organised in north Wales, objected to what seemed like a loose operation tied to local forces that weren't able to see the 'big picture'. Surely, the Met argued, any large-scale intelligence-led operation should come under the guidance of the 'specialists' of the Central Drugs Intelligence Unit. The meeting decided to refer the matter back to the chief constables of the various forces, which usually meant that nothing more would be heard of it. Fortunately for Lee, he was supported by Philip Myers, chief constable of North Wales and Richard Thomas, chief constable of Dyfed Powys, As a result, a national squad, based in Devizes, Wiltshire, was formed, and given the code-name, Operation Julie. DCI George Herbert of Avon and Somerset was appointed as executive commander, and Lee as operational commander of the squad of twenty-six detectives, which included four undercover officers. Herbert took charge of getting various police forces to loan out vehicles and radios, but he found the vehicles to be inadequate and the car-to-car frequency on the radios so close to Capitol Radio that they could be overheard. For his troubles Herbert was pulled from the squad by his superiors and, much to Lee's fury, sent back to Avon and Somerset. Herbert was replaced by Detective Superintendent Dennis Greenslade who, according to Stephen Bentley, was a 'glory hunter', placed at the top of the Operation Julie command structure 'to spy on Lee on behalf of the establishment'.

Once Operation Julie was launched, Lee appealed to higher authority to get the Central Drugs Intelligence Unit to hand over their files on LSD. When they were released to him it then became obvious why the CDIU had not wanted anyone else to see them:

> For they contained a number of leads pointing to an LSD conspiracy in the United Kingdom, but unfortunately the information had been in the hands of the unit for two years and almost nothing was done about it... the information had been withheld from all drug squads except the Metropolitan, and when they failed to act on it, no one else had the chance.

From the CDIU files Lee learned that after Gerald Thomas was busted for hash-smuggling in Montreal in 1973, he told Canadian police that he knew of a major LSD production ring in Britain. The Canadian police passed on details of his confession to the Central Drugs Intelligence Unit in London. In April 1974 Detective Inspectors Derek Godfrey and Charles O'Hanlon of the Met flew to Montreal to interview Thomas. Thomas named Richard Kemp, Christine Bott, David Solomon and a man he simply knew as 'Henry' as the leaders of the ring. He gave them Solomon's London address in Randolph Avenue and told them that Bott was a doctor living with Kemp somewhere in London. He revealed that Kemp stored his lab equipment in Bristol and that production usually took place early in the year so they could distribute the LSD at summer pop festivals. Solomon, who Thomas said was 'connected' to Timothy Leary and the Brotherhood of Eternal Love, was the procurer of ergotamine tartrate and other chemicals from West Germany, using the alias, 'Dr Andressen'. Solomon sold the finished product of LSD to an (unnamed) contact in Amsterdam. Thomas said he had met George Andrews, Solomon's author friend, at a London flat owned by 'Henry'. Solomon was 'a member of an exclusive intellectual circle surrounding Dr Ronald D Laing, a 'top psychiatrist in London's Harley St'. Richard Kemp was 'a political extremist intent on causing revolution by wide distribution of LSD'. Christine Bott, who also attended RD Laing's seminars, shared Kemp's philosophy on drugs. 'Henry' was in charge of tableting and distribution.

Shortly after Godfrey and O'Hanlon returned from Canada in 1974, O'Hanlon was suspended and subsequently sentenced to eight years imprisonment for receiving corrupt payments from pornographers during an earlier stint with the Metropolitan Obscene Publications Squad. At this time the Met's own drug squad was reeling from a corruption scandal which resulted in a number of them being sacked or 'retired' and six officers going to prison for taking payments from cannabis dealers. Lee mentions £10,000 in bribes paid by an Anglo-Dutch drugs ring to British police officers between 1971 and 1974 to ensure those charged could get out on bail and 'disappear'. Worse still, all of the files on the Anglo-Dutch investigation had been destroyed.

DI Derek Godfrey, according to Lee's undercover officer, Stephen Bentley, was the 'only Metropolitan police officer Lee trusted'. It was Godfrey who initiated an investigation of David Solomon's trip to Switzerland in 1972 for a meeting with Timothy Leary to help secure a publishing deal for a book about his life on-the-run, entitled *Confessions of Hope Fiend*. Godfrey, on his return from Canada in 1974, tried to follow up Thomas's information. He couldn't trace Kemp and Bott but he did learn that in May 1970 Kemp was checked by Dover police entering the country from France with Simon Walton, who was found to have convictions for heroin possession. The Ferrari, it had been noted, was owned by a Dr Ronald Stark, who after the DEA raids in 1972 on the Brotherhood of Eternal Love, was now an indicted fugitive.

In early 1975, the Metropolitan Police had put a tap on the telephone of David Solomon at Randolph Avenue. The Met, as Lee put it, then 'botched' a raid on Solomon's home and failed to find anything incriminating. The Met didn't know where Kemp was but his name was entered into their checking system and flagged as a 'person of interest'. A potential breakthrough came with the tragic motor accident in April, after which Kemp's Range Rover was impounded by the police. Gerald Thomas had correctly identified Kemp's car as a red Range Rover. A thorough search of the vehicle yielded a torn up map of various locations and a torn up piece of paper bearing the words 'hydrazine hydrate'. Lee, after consulting Home Office scientists, designated hydrazine hydrate as 'an essential ingredient in the manufacture of LSD'. In fact it isn't essential for LSD manufacture at all, but as Andy Roberts suggests, this was a case of ignorance is bliss on Lee's part: 'it set him on the right track, for the wrong reasons'.

Kemp had been obliged to give his current address at Penlleinau, which enabled the police to place a tap on his telephone. The taps yielded nothing of interest; Solomon, having been raided by the police, was now cautious about his phone conversations; and Kemp was too distressed by the road accident to talk business. The phone taps were removed and Godfrey was instructed to hand over the case to the Welsh regional crime squad. The local police found themselves unable to mount a surveillance of Kemp and Bott's cottage, which was isolated and had a splendid view over the surrounding area.

*

Now that Operation Julie was up and running with a full squad of detectives, Inspector Lee approached officials in the Home Office, and requested an expensive tracking device to install in Kemp's Renault on the grounds that some of the acidheads possibly had 'terrorist connections'. Lee says in his book, *Operation Julie, How the Undercover Police Team Smashed the World's Greatest Drugs Gang* (1978), that his surveillance teams came across possible connections between the LSD networks and organised terrorism. He records that one of his target's description was 'similar to that of a German who was a *suspected* member of the Baader-Meinhof gang... known to have stayed at an isolated cottage near Warminster, Wiltshire which was also visited by *other* members of the Baader-Meinhof gang...' (emphases mine) – a rather loose claim, to say the least. Worse still, he put one Peter John Panting in the frame as a both an associate of the Microdot Gang and Bott, and an 'associate of the Angry Brigade, the group responsible for bomb outrages in Britain three years earlier.' Panting, a school laboratory assistant in Tregaron, who happened to have met Kemp and Bott, sued Lee's publishers, WH Allen. Panting was awarded a thousand pounds in compensation and the publishers were ordered to put an errata slip expunging the libel in all remaining copies of the book. The Free Wales Army was also mentioned as having some support amongst the drug dealers, but in fact the Free Wales Army had been defunct since the imprisonment of its leadership back in 1969. Lee's request for James Bond-grade surveillance gadgets was rejected by the Home Office officials he approached. As gatekeepers for MI5 they were not convinced by Lee's hyperbole and conspiracy theorising; and in any case regarded 'National Security' as the domain of the intelligence services and Special Branch, not the dope-squad.

Lee was loath to use regular police channels to obtain telephone taps of suspects in London, because he thought corrupt Met officers might be leaking information to the targets. Having gotten little from the security services Lee turned to the Investigation Division of Her Majesty's Customs and Excise. One of its elite units, known as Alpha, was able to provide Lee with intelligence picked up from their own telephone interceptions and high-tech bugging devices. According to Peter Walsh's book, *Drug War: The Secret History*

> Alpha's expertise lay behind the success in 1977 of Operation Julie... The lead officer, DI Dick Lee, wanted to tap the phone of a leading participant, Henry Todd, but was loath to follow protocol and use Scotland Yard because he feared a leak; an informant had claimed that the gang was bribing certain London cops. Instead Lee turned to what he later described as 'an organisation which for security reasons cannot be named'. It was Alpha... Alpha was able to identify important locations and personnel. The listener in charge would meet a police officer to pass on information but refused to give transcripts... Amid a welter of publicity at the trial's conclusion, the role of HMCE was barely mentioned – which was just how they wanted it.

When, in May 1976, Lee went to San Francisco to interview Gerald Thomas, he was informed of further links in the chain, namely Andrew Munro, who was identified as a chemist, and Paul Arnaboldi, who was described as another one-time associate of Timothy Leary. By this time surveillance of Kemp by the Julie squad had already revealed he was meeting Arnaboldi at Plas Llysin in Carno.

The grounds of the Plas Llysin mansion house were surrounded by a high wall. A stream flowed through the grounds. There were no hills or buildings overlooking the property, which made close surveillance impossible. Plas Llysin was watched by a team of detectives lodged in a caravan, pretending to be surveyors looking for possible coal seams in the area. Through binoculars and infra-red cameras, the team was able to monitor visitors to the mansion. They observed visits by Richard Kemp in a car driven by Christine Bott, who would return 48 hours later to take him back to Penlleinau. Another visitor to Plas Llysin who was an American called Vladimir Petroff-Tchomakov, who had jumped bail on LSD charges in the US. Soon afterwards Petroff-Tchomakov left the mansion and disappeared, never to be seen again. Then Arnaboldi was seen loading suitcases into his car and driving away, bound for Majorca. Lee realised that – while the place was being watched – a production run seemed to have already been completed. And so it had. Arnaboldi had left Plas Llysin with a flask containing millions of doses of LSD. There was no attempt to stop him at Southampton where he boarded the Bilbao ferry, though he was placed on a watchlist. What was Lee to do now the acid had left the building? How was he going to locate all of the LSD produced at Plas Llysin before it could be distributed? Where was it being tableted? If Kemp had finished with the lab at Plas Lysin, was a new one being planned for the next production run? If so, where?

In the meantime Lee decided on a break-in at the now unoccupied Plas Llysin mansion and brought in chemists from the Aldermaston military research centre to conduct tests for traces of LSD. After forcing an entry his team found traces of chemicals related to LSD production in the cellar. A dead mole in the drains was found to have died from LSD poisoning. It was also found that the usage of water – some half a million gallons – was ten times that of the average property of that size would normally use.

Meanwhile, the Penlleinau cottage where Kemp was tableting his LSD was being watched through telescopes by a team of detectives in a holiday cottage 200 yards away. A hidden cable, run from a transmitter on top of a mountain a mile away to a microphone in the garden wall, malfunctioned after it was chewed by a passing sheep. Lee, once again playing his ill-founded 'terrorist connections' card, asked the Home Office for a tracking device to place on Kemp's car, and for a bug to be placed inside the Penlleinau residence. Both requests were turned down.

Taking advantage of a ladder and a left-open window, officers sneaked illegally into Kemp and Bott's home when they were out and found evidence of tableting taking place on the premises. Surveillance of the cottage showed visits from Mark Tcharney and his partner Hilary Rees, who were followed by the surveillance team to their house in Esgarwein, Uchaf. Mark and Hilary were seen working on 'improvements' to their property which indicated to Lee that they might be preparing a new laboratory.

Operation Julie had identified the nucleus of Kemp's operation and his laboratory at Plas Llysin. But by May 1976, Kemp's LSD was either in circulation or stashed for future distribution. The police now had enough evidence to arrest him there and then, but they decided to run the risk that he might flee the country, until they could take down his distributors as well. But unknown to the police, there were two distribution networks; each supplied by two separate labs and operating quite separately from each other, despite having common origins.

*

In the summer of 1975, a few months after the botched raid on Alston 'Smiles' Hughes at Llanddewi Brefi, undercover officer Martyn Pritchard was able to confirm that two LSD dealers in Wiltshire – John McDonnell and William Lochhead – were getting their supplies from Llanddewi Brefi. As it was apparent that the April raid hadn't rendered Hughes inactive, a tap was placed on his telephone, and undercover officers Stephen Bentley and Eric Wright were assigned to infiltrate Hughes' milieu.

Bentley and Wright presented themselves at Llanddewi Brefi as odd-job men, who made a living from cutting trees with a chain saw they kept in their van. They took up residence, first in a caravan nearby, then in a flat in the village. As they had to frequently liaise with the Operation Julie HQ in Devizes, they had to explain their absences. Their cover-story was that they frequently travelled around the country to buy and sell second-hand; and that they were looking for a long-lost kid brother of Wright's, who had gone missing and was believed to be living with hippies somewhere in the Welsh mountains. A likely story? Perhaps. Bentley and Wright, who spent months of heavy drinking, smoking hash and occasionally snorting coke in the company of Smiles and his friends, convinced themselves that their target harboured no suspicions that they were undercover cops. Smiles for his part, is adamant that he knew all along. Andy Roberts writes:

> Smiles, in 2016, told me of his initial meeting with Bentley, 'Anyway, these two herberts walk in. Instinctively I knew they were cops and said, 'what'll it be officers? Two halves as you're on duty' and considers their flustered retorts, the exact words of which he has forgotten, to have confirmed his instinct.

Stephen Bentley (alias the hippie, Steve Jackson) rejects this anecdote as 'second hand hearsay'. As his rejection is insistent; and since he was 'there', his comments to me are worth quoting at length:

> Perhaps he did say that to Roberts. But it's not true and that's why it irks me to see this story of Smiles repeated in books concerning Operation Julie. Please allow me to show you why Smiles' story is a face-saving fabrication and one that I feel compelled to discredit...

To give a few examples,

> Why didn't Smiles warn anyone in the drug distribution network? Clearly, he didn't as the telephone intercepts would surely have disclosed the warning. Why didn't that intercept record any suspicions he harboured about Eric (my undercover partner) and me?... Why did he supply Jackson [Bentley] with cannabis and

cocaine? Why give Jackson a Christmas gift of cannabis? Why were Jackson and Walker (Eric Wright's undercover name) frequent welcome and invited guests in his home? Why did Smiles choose to be a regular heavy-session drinking buddy of Jackson?... Why did he often talk about drug dealing with Jackson? Why has he made claims that he was told of Jackson's identity and yet did nothing about it?

It should have been evident to Hughes, following the failed raid on his house, that the police would come after him again if he was still dealing – which he was. It seems likely that Hughes did know they were undercover cops, and that rather than call them out he found it more expedient to pretend he believed them. But keeping your enemies closer than your friends is a dangerous game if you don't know what your enemies really have on you and what they might do if you expose them. In his book, Steve Bentley reflects at length on the psychological stress he experienced in being 'Steve Jackson' and fearing exposure every waking minute. Such alcohol-fuelled stress could cause volatile behaviour. Douglas Flannagan, a dealer associate of Hughes, was pushed through a shop window when blind drunk by Bentley, so he could be arrested and forced to supply his address in London. Neither Flannagan nor Hughes suspected Bentley as being responsible for pulling this dangerous stunt. Eric Wright as 'Eric Walker' had threatened Hughes with a beating after he made one joke too many about the pair being undercover cops. Hopefully Smiles will shed further light on the matter in his forthcoming memoirs.

It is certainly striking that the principals of the British acid underground were in almost universal denial about being watched and investigated, despite numerous indicators: the botched raids on the homes of Solomon in London and Hughes in Wales, which found nothing; police radio messages which could be heard on FM radios and jukeboxes; suspicious signs of surveillance; the assault on Flannagan; tip-offs from landlords about police enquiries; and Welsh locals gossiping about 'hippie cops'.

*

The Julie squad followed up on Gerald Thomas' testament regarding a principal conspirator known only as 'Henry'. Having heard reports of a 'Henry' in Solomon's circle in Cambridge, they checked all the 'Henrys' in local police files on drugs and found that the name 'Henry Barclay Todd' kept coming up. Todd was then traced to an address on Cannon Street Road, east London. This however, was just an accommodation address, therefore a blind alley. Next, the police laboriously trawled through records in various government departments but found that Todd used the same Cannon Street address every time. The breakthrough came when they found a passport application Henry Todd had put in for his daughter on which he'd entered his telephone number. The number was traced to Todd's home at 29 Fitzgeorge Ave, near Olympia. The Julie squad, having located Todd, put him under heavy surveillance and tapped his telephone. A motorised surveillance team followed him driving to Seymour Rd. A watch on the house revealed that Cuthbertson and Munro were regular visitors. The squad also discovered that Cuthbertson knew Leaf Fielding in Reading, who they had already tied in with Spenceley and Hughes in Wales through telephone taps. According to Martyn Pritchard: 'The obs team checked all three guys [Todd, Munro and Cuthbertson] into the house... They stayed locked in there for three days, and when they reappeared it was very clear as they walked down the road that Munro was tripping.' When the suspects took rubbish to the municipal dump, the detectives retrieved the bags, tested the contents and found traces of incriminating chemicals. To Pritchard all this suggested that the three targets were running a lab on the premises. His boss, Richard Lee, rejected this as a possibility, preferring to believe in one big centralised conspiracy of international dimensions. Lee had no idea that the distribution network centred on Llanddewi Brefi was quite unconnected with Kemp's chemistry work taking place just a few miles away. Neither did anyone in Alston Hughes' network know about it, as their supplies of LSD came from Henry Todd's lab in London via Leaf Fielding and Russell Spenceley.

14 – Downfall

The principals of the LSD networks were racing against time, hoping they could sell their acid, take the money and run. But it was too late. Thirteen months on from the launch of Operation Julie, Lee was finally ready to strike. On 26 March 1977, 800 police officers were mobilised to arrest 130 people in a nationwide round-up of suspects at 87 different premises. Richard Kemp reflected:

> When we were busted frankly I was not surprised. We had had many warnings in the previous couple of years but I had rationalised them all the way. After living with the tension of dangers of this project for 8 or 9 years one's ability to react in the presence of danger deteriorates. Even when Christine Bott was picked up by the Swiss police with £16,000 we managed to convince ourselves it was a coincidence and carried on as if nothing had happened.

Within hours of the raids the Operation Julie squad was telling the media that they had achieved an historic breakthrough in the war on drugs. In truth it was also a day of disappointments. Of the millions of acid tabs from the two labs that had gone into circulation in the past year not a lot were found in the raids. A raid on Paul Arnaboldi's London address in Belsize Gardens failed to find any trace of him. He had left for Spain the previous day. The high point as regards seizure of LSD was 50,000 microdots found in Tony Dalton's flat in Georgiana

Street, London. In Lee's account of the raid on Seymour Road, as well as £20,000 in cash, 'they found 250 milligrammes of pure LSD. Enough to make 2,500,000 microdots'. In fact 250 milligrammes equals a quarter of a gram, which would make 2,000 tabs at the most. In Martin Annable's house in London 26,000 Dutch guilders were seized. Around the country numerous suspected acid dealers were raided, but many were caught in possession of varying amounts of cannabis, not LSD. At the same time, at Lee's request, Brian Cuthbertson's chateau at Périgueux in the Dordogne was raided by the French drug squad. Lee had suspected that the chateau might be housing a laboratory, but it wasn't and there was no LSD to be found there. However, Dai Rees, a Welsh drug squad officer Lee sent to liaise with the gendarmes, did find bank documents and a Swiss safe deposit box key relating to Cuthbertson's assets in Switzerland. Izchak Sheni AKA 'Zahi', the Israeli who distributed both Kemp's LSD (supplied by David Solomon) and Munro's LSD (supplied by Richard Burden) through Amsterdam was missed. When the Julie Squad checked his London address they found he had left the country. In the raid on Tcharney's house at Esgarwein, they were disappointed to find there was no evidence of a lab being built for Kemp's next production run.

Despite the mixed success of the raids, in the post-arrest interrogations over the next few weeks, the principals of the two microdot gangs and those in the distribution chains realised that the police had gathered enough incriminating evidence to convict virtually all of them. As several of the defendants' wives and girlfriends had been caught up in the swoop and were facing possible prison sentences, there was pressure on the men to confess and co-operate. The defendants also hoped – largely in vain – that giving up large stashes of acid might get them shorter sentences. Leaf Fielding agreed to show Bentley and Pritchard his stash in the woods of over a hundred thousand microdots, which they celebrated as a 'world record breaker'. The record was again broken when Brian Cuthbertson and Henry Todd accompanied Lee and other detectives to the woods in search of a large stash. 670,000 microdots, sealed in plastic containers, were dug up. Christine Bott offered to show the police what she and Kemp had buried in the garden at their cottage. Bott's day out in her old garden yielded the tableting boards for LSD plus some brown bottles containing 120 grams of pure LSD crystal. She also signed a statement of authority to allow police to access her safe deposit box at the Kantonal Bank in Zurich which contained bonds and cash in various currencies worth in all about £60,000. Mark Tcharney gave up a stash of 50,000 tabs.

Fielding recalls that Andy Munro, in a prison conversation, claimed he warned the squad not to touch a carpet that had been rolled up in the lab at Seymour Road after he spilled a flask of LSD on it containing 150,000 trips. Munro claimed that the warning was ignored and three officers who examined the carpet were heavily dosed with LSD. According to Fielding, one of the officers told him just how good the experience had been until he and his colleagues were hauled off for 'psychiatric' treatment at a Kingston Hospital. (In my previous book,

Psychedelic Tricksters (2020) I wrongly attributed the warning about the contaminated carpet to Leaf Fielding, who was told the story by Andy Munro.)

Inspector Lee believed that despite Kemp's declaration of independence from Stark, his LSD production and distribution ring was the 'British connection' of the Brotherhood of Eternal Love. The three Americans involved with Kemp — David Solomon, Paul Arnaboldi, and Gerry Thomas — had been associated with Timothy Leary's Millbrook centre. The US Drug Enforcement Agency regarded Leary as the 'Guru' of the Brotherhood, which to Lee suggested that Solomon, Arnaboldi, and Thomas were members 'of the inner circle of the Brotherhood'. Lee found that 'in the years between 1967 and 1972 the Brotherhood had set up the British connection through Druce and Craze in London [and] had financed Alban Feeds and Inland Alkaloids to supply ergotamine tartrate'. Also, he noted, 'major Brotherhood figures such as Stark, Sand and Hitchcock, who were regular visitors to Britain, had been associated with Timothy Leary's Millbrook centre.' Lee believed that the Brotherhood of Eternal Love was an organisational continuation of Leary's League of Spiritual discovery, and that the Microdot Gang was a continuation of the Brotherhood in transatlantic form. It is true that Leary, as a friend of the Brotherhood's founder John Griggs, formally 'blessed' the group when it registered as church in 1966. But it was only in late-1968 that Tim Scully recruited the Brotherhood to distribute the Orange Sunshine LSD he and Nick Sand were making; a move which enabled them to avoid using the Hell's

Angels as distributors. Leary had no knowledge of this arrangement or of Ron Stark, who didn't meet the Brotherhood of Eternal Love until 1970 – by which time he was already working with Richard Kemp in Paris. Furthermore, Stark's association with the Brotherhood – which was essentially an amorphous organization of subgroups – was limited to a few members of its LSD subsystem and particularly with Michael Randall (who succeeded the late John Griggs as leader).

One of the reasons Lee delayed the big bust was his mistaken theory that Kemp was building labs at Tcharney's house in Wales and Cuthbertson's chateau in France. Another was his refusal to believe that Todd's organisation was anything more than a distribution network until he walked into the fully functioning laboratory at Todd's premises in Seymour Road.

Independently of Kemp's operation, the trio of Todd, Munro and Cuthbertson had, in the previous two years, made an estimated 30 million microdots from 15 kilos of ergotamine tartrate. Following the arrests, the police calculated there were about fifteen million trips stashed or still in circulation. According to Fielding, this was an exaggeration; there was only about half that amount. Whatever, this was a problem for the police as they had been in a position to bust the production labs for several months but had held off to investigate the distribution chains. Leaf Fielding says that the 'tall tales' spread by the police about the 'killer drug' LSD also served to 'obscure the embarrassing fact that they'd watched us for years while we made and distributed millions of LSD tablets... and had signally failed to find the bulk of our acid'.

Stephen Bentley offers a differing opinion, referring to 'Fielding's inane point about the Julie squad permitting them all to continue distributing LSD until the busts in March 1977 after we had tracked Kemp to the Welsh lab in May 1976'. Bentley insists: 'That was the brief: to take out the manufacturing *and* distribution networks. The latter took time and the gathering of a mountain of evidence through surveillance.'

Certainly, after a year's work, Operation Julie was successful in arresting the principals of the London lab and their network. Detectives and undercover officers doggedly and laboriously investigated the network from the ground up, which resulted in the prosecution of dozens of sub-distributors, as well as Todd, Cuthbertson and Munro. But in that year the London gang had shifted millions of LSD tabs.

As regards the lab in Wales, only the principals Kemp, Bott, Solomon and Tcharney were caught. Paul Arnaboldi left Wales for Spain in May 1976 with millions of trips worth of LSD crystals and escaped the Julie raids as well In Majorca, Arnaboldi was arrested by Spanish police at the request of the Julie squad but as there was no extradition treaty between Spain and Britain he was released. He took a plane to New York, where he was arrested but released pending lengthy extradition proceedings. He then flew to Florida and disappeared. Izchak Sheni disappeared along with his Amsterdam-based distribution network. Though he is mentioned only in passing in Lee's book, he was clearly the most important international distributor, not only of Kemp's microdots, but also Munro's.

*

After the Julie bust, in the year before trial, Kemp met Solomon in prison in Bristol, where the principals of the two gangs were all held on remand. Solomon complained he wouldn't have been charged if Kemp and Mark Tcharney hadn't talked to the police about what they'd been doing and who else they'd been working with. Solomon was hauled in after someone in Tcharney's house, telephoned his London number and said, 'Mark's been arrested. Expect trouble', then hung up. As there was a tap on Tcharney's phone, the call was traced to Solomon's London address. Inspector Lee later told Steve Abrams that they had very little evidence on David Solomon: he never visited Penlleinau, and none of his sub-distributors were identified (apart from Sheni who was never traced). Lee told Abrams that if only Solomon had kept his mouth shut in response to police questioning he would have escaped conviction.

As far as Kemp was concerned, it was pointless for any of them to deny the mass of evidence the police had gathered on what they had been doing for last nine years. With his fellow prisoners he discussed an alternative strategy of defence, based on good will and compromise. The police would easily discover from the Renschler company records that 9 kilos of ergotamine tartrate had been purchased to be converted into millions of LSD doses. Kemp pointed out in a later statement:

I could only account for 3 kilos of the 9 in my statement and it was very clear that the Judge would be persuaded by forensic experts that we probably had a large quantity of LSD stashed somewhere and would sentence accordingly. I discussed this in general terms with other members of the group and I decided the best thing would be to reveal to the judge himself the existence and whereabouts of this LSD. I thought this tactic would be advantageous. I thought it would go a long way to mitigating our crimes for everybody if the Judge felt that I had voluntarily handed over this material, it would also suggest that we had no intention of continuing with our illegal activities. I told Solomon this is what I decided to do and he was a bit annoyed. He said we had handed over too much already and that I should say I made a mess of the process and got a low yield or something. I said I didn't think anyone would believe this and that what was most important to me was my freedom and not a couple of pounds of white powder. He agreed and said of course the final decision on what to do must rest with me but he was against any more handovers.

Encased in concrete under a stove at Kemp's cottage in Wales was a box containing 1.2 kilos of pure LSD crystal, enough for six million trips, with a sell-by date well into the next century. Police searches of his property had missed it. But Kemp's plan to use the secret stash of six million LSD trips as a bargaining chip unravelled on 1 December 1977, eight months after the arrests, when the Julie squad, acting on 'information received', dug up Kemp's kitchen floor and found his flask of LSD crystal. According to Leaf Fielding, 'With promises of preferential treatment they persuaded one of Richard's lieutenants to go to work for them. The turncoat was able to worm out the location of Richard's stash.' A plea bargain deal with the turncoat was approved by the Home Secretary. The identity of the snitch may possibly lie in a Home Office file that is locked until the year 2062.

Kemp clearly thought at the time that Solomon was the snitch. Kemp claimed that '[Solomon] continued to press me where the LSD was stashed and in the end I told him it was under the floor of my cottage and told him exactly where.' If Solomon did reveal the stash as a plea bargain, he didn't get a very good deal, as he ended up with a stiff ten-year sentence. The only other principal defendants Kemp and Bott dealt with directly were the courier, Mark Tcharney, who got a three-year sentence, and Paul Arnaboldi, who evaded extradition from the US, became a fugitive and died a free man in Mexico forty years later.

Kemp alleged that Solomon's statement to the police was a pack of 'outright lies'. In it Solomon claimed that it was Kemp who suggested making LSD back in 1968, whereas, as Nick Green could testify, it had been the other way around. Solomon tried to throw the whole responsibility for distribution through Izchak 'Zahi' Sheni onto Mark Tcharney. According to Solomon, Tcharney had on one occasion travelled to Amsterdam to meet

Solomon at Sheni's flat to 'organise distribution'. But, according to Kemp, Tcharney's role had simply been to deliver LSD to Solomon, collect the sales-money and deliver it to Kemp – all by means of dead-letter drops. Solomon also denied all knowledge of Gerald Thomas despite the fact that it was he who had introduced Thomas to Kemp. Kemp sought to counter Solomon's allegations and show that if anyone in the conspiracy was the 'mastermind' it was Solomon. Solomon told the police that he'd never had any pecuniary motive for distributing LSD. Again, Kemp contradicted this. The bottom line was that he, Kemp, was no longer a practising criminal trying to make money out of drugs. Kemp went on:

> In contrast I understand Solomon is in direct contact with the dealer Zahi and has been receiving money from him since he has been in prison. I believe this money has been routed through his daughter Kim's British bank account and that he stands to get 50,000 dollars for the last 100,000 tablets which were given to Zahi just before the bust. I believe he has already received about £7,000.

Kemp having, as he thought, been played a fool by Solomon, tried a 'Plan B'. Kemp wrote a 15,000-word counter-narrative – some of which has been quoted above – as a 'full and frank' account of the acid adventure he had been involved in for the last nine years. His 'Voluntary Statement of Richard Hilary Kemp' was handed to Detective Superintendent Greenslade at Horsfield Prison, Bristol on Friday, 30 December 1977.

In his account Kemp names names, often deliberately misspelled to invalidate the references as potential evidence in court. Kemp, however, refers seemingly to everyone he ever worked with on LSD, including the minor players. This was a final, desperate, plea-bargaining ploy. By coming clean about his own historical role at the top of the conspiracy and portraying himself as the idealistic leader who thought making money from acid was just a 'necessary evil', he may have thought he could get a lighter sentence and that this would help his co-defendants in the sense of the old aphorism: 'a rising tide lifts all boats'. But, deprived of his bargaining ploy to voluntarily hand over his stash of acid he could only throw himself and his co-defendants on the mercy of the court. He wrote to Greenslade, pleadingly:

> I realise that it is hard to expect anyone to believe that it was my intention to hand over this material but my legal advisers had already told me that if there was any LSD outstanding of which I knew it should be handed over. I could only repeat sincerely that it was my intention to reveal its whereabouts to the judge at the trial where I thought it would have the maximum impact. I would like to add that my present circumstances are as follows: I have no hidden stash of LSD or money. I have no secret bank accounts in any foreign country. I have no valuable assets such as jewellery, coins or stamps. I own no property or even a motor car. My total worldly possession is the £10 I have in the canteen

account at Horsley Prison. When I am released from prison I'll have nothing to come out to whatsoever.

Kemp's confession did him no good, and didn't figure in the evidence presented by either side in court. The British establishment was in no mood for mercy or appeals to non-pecuniary motives such as 'idealism'.

There were a few voices of dissent in the mainstream media. One of them, 'Dick Tracy' (John May) in the *New Musical Express* (*NME*) commented:

> It has been standard practice in the British and American media for many years now to distort the true nature of the drug LSD. Medical research into the subject has been officially frowned on, but nevertheless there is a considerable body of evidence available, enough to refute most of the basic untruths. Needless to say, medical facts were ignored in favour of selling newspapers. Operation Julie provided the press with a field day, allowing them to dust off all the old cliches and trot them out into print.

The article was well-placed, in that the *NME* at the time was the paper most favoured by punk rockers, many of whom tended to hold 'old hippies' in contempt.

On 8 March 1978, 29 defendants were handed down prison sentences totalling 170 years. The sentences for the principal defendants amounted to 133 years. The disparity in the numbers of prosecutions between the two gangs is noteworthy:

In the Kemp group:

Richard Kemp (33): 13 years.

David Solomon (52): 10 years.

Dr Christine Bott (32): 9 years.

Dr Mark Tcharney (24): 3 years.

In the Todd group:

Henry Barclay Todd (32), formerly Kemp's marketing manager, later in charge of the laboratory at Seymour Road, London: 10 years.

Brian Cuthbertson (28) Todd's marketing manager: 11 years.

Dr Andrew Munro (29) Todd's chemist: 10 years.

Russell Spenceley (27) major distributor: 10 years.

Nigel 'Leaf' Fielding (29) Todd's chief distributor: 8 years.

Alston 'Smiles' Hughes (30) major distributor based in Llanddewi Brefi, Wales: 8 years.

William Lochhead, distributor: 8 years.

John Preece, distributor: 8 years.

Martin Annable (29), cash-handler: 6 years.

Richard Burden (26), distributor for London and Amsterdam: 6 years.

David Brown Todd (23), Henry Todd's brother and helper: 6 years.

Anthony Dalton (32) distributor: 5 years.

Douglas Flannagan (28) distributor: 2 years.

Others in the Todd chain of distribution charged with lesser offences got lighter prison sentences. These included Christopher Casa-Grande and Mostyn Crewe (1 year each); and Paul 'Buzz' Healy, who was Alston Hughes chauffeur (1 year). Several busted in the big raids in possession of cannabis were contacts of Hughes who had been smuggling hash from Morocco, namely: John Heasman, 2 years; David Robertson and Nicolas Pelopida, 4 years each; and Christopher Osborne and Gordon Evans, 2 years each.

Monica Kenyon (Tony Dalton's girlfriend) and Janine Spenceley admitted 'participation' in their partners dealing, and walked with 2-year suspended sentences. In contrast Christine Bott carried a copy of Timothy Leary's *Politics of Ecstasy* around with her during the trial, and refused to pretend she had been pressurised by Kemp or had 'turned a blind eye' to his activities. Bott was one of only three defendants to plead not guilty. She spoke from the dock about the positive aspects of LSD use. 'If I thought there was a crime,' she said. 'I thought it had more to do with making money than making LSD.' Justice Park handed her a cruel and unjust sentence of nine years. Andrew Munro commented, 'Bott got nine years for making sandwiches. I got ten years for making acid' – which was true insofar as Bott had not actually participated in the manufacture or distribution of LSD, though she had helped out with moving money and ergotamine tartrate through Swiss bank accounts and deposit boxes.

It was claimed by detective constable Martyn Pritchard that, as a result of Operation Julie, the price of LSD skyrocketed from £1 to £8 a tab. This was contradicted by a report issued by the Release organisation, stating that at the Glastonbury Festival in 1981, it was being sold for £1.50 a tab. Acid imported from the US compensated for the lost British production. The *Mirror* claimed that the gang's turnover in 1976 alone was £200 million. This figure was contradicted by a defence lawyer, who estimated that the total profits of the syndicates from start to finish amounted to around £700,000.

*

As the Operation Julie investigation was winding down, Detective Chief Inspector Richard Lee contacted RD Laing and Steve Abrams through Bing Spear at the Home Office to suggest a 'social' get-together. Lee and Sergeant Allen Buxton came round to Laing's home and announced that although both Laing and Abrams had been 'in the frame' at one stage in the investigation, they were now happily off the hook. The police had been interested in Abrams and Laing because both of them had been associates of David Solomon. Gerald Thomas had told Canadian police that Solomon, 'was a member of an exclusive intellectual circle surrounding Dr Ronald D Laing, a top psychiatrist', and that Christine Bott had attended Laing's seminars. That apparently had been enough for the Metropolitan Police drug squad to arrest RD Laing in 1977. According to Steve Abrams, Lee told Laing that the Met had been acting independently of his operation and that someone in the Met had it in for the doctor:

> I remember Laing calling me up to say he had been arrested; he stayed the night and then went off to court with me the next morning. He was saying, "but I'm a famous psychiatrist, they can't do this to me".

The Metropolitan Police had seized about 150 bottles of Czechoslovak LSD, each containing small one-dose units of 150 μg. These had been supplied to Laing on license by the Ministry of Health to use with his patients, so he was in legal possession. Also the LSD in the bottles turned out to be inert due to age; Laing had forgotten about them. The case against him was dropped and he was awarded £500 costs.

Inspector Lee wanted Laing to explain how such intelligent people as those he had just put behind bars could have become involved with the LSD trade. During a heavy whisky-drinking session, a lively and frank conversation ensued about psychiatry and the politics of LSD and cannabis, in which the officers were thoroughly briefed on what Abrams and Laing saw as the dysfunctional and unworkable drugs policy of the Government. As Lee and Buxton staggered into the night, arguing amongst themselves, Abrams and Laing mimicked the parliamentary chant: 'Resign! Resign!' Abrams got a telephone call late the next afternoon telling him that Lee and his driver had both resigned from the police force - as did several other officers of the Julie Squad.

There was a lot of bad feeling among the Julie squad's members over the lack of recognition for their work. Holding the main trial at Bristol Crown Court rather than the Old Bailey in

London ensured it was denied the world media attention the officers thought it deserved. Despite the success of Operation Julie in smashing the British acid underground, Richard Lee and many of his officers felt that the 'establishment' had deliberately frustrated any proper investigation of the 'international connections' – some of which Lee suspected may have involved terrorists and/or foreign intelligence agencies.

Stephen Bentley describes Lee as 'devious', in that he 'would play both parties or all of the parties if it suited his ends... an intelligent man, yet sometimes he came out with ridiculous ideas. Dick Lee loved a good conspiracy theory.' Nevertheless, echoing Lee's resentment at being blocked from on high from investigating Stark and other overseas trails, Bentley writes,

> Clearly Stark was worthy of investigation by the Operation Julie team. He was never interviewed by us. Dick Lee sought permission to go to the Rome prison where Stark was serving his sentence to interview him. He got short shrift – that was beyond the remit of Operation Julie! Another piece of unfinished business was the Israeli Izchak Sheni. He was known as Zani to us on the Operation Julie team as that was how he was known to Mark Tcharney and Solomon. Zani was a dealer in heroin and LSD based in Amsterdam. He supplied drugs to Israel and other countries worldwide. One source of information was adamant that he supplied Mossad, the Israeli secret police. The informant noted that Mossad in turn supplied the CIA with some of this

LSD. Solomon used Tcharney as a courier to deliver the Kemp acid to Zani in Amsterdam. The remit for Operation Julie was to bring the manufacturers and distribution network to justice. Zani was key player in that distribution network. At one stage in the investigation Lee was as excited about this dealer as any other, if not more so. For some reason that excitement waned and Zani seemed to be a forgotten link. My own thoughts on that? Lee was warned off by the security services either in Britain or overseas.

Sheni/Zani disappeared at the time of Operation Julie's climax; he and the possible Mossad or CIA connection remains a complete mystery. We do, however, know what became of Ronald Hadley Stark.

15 – Trickster

In February 1975, the Bologna Carabiniere, acting on tip-off about a stolen cars racket, raided a room at the Grand Hotel Baglioni. When they searched the room they discovered several kilos of cannabis, a small quantity of morphine and cocaine, a large sum of money in foreign currencies and a key for a safe deposit box in Rome. Three people present were arrested: Franco Buda, an Italian who procured stolen cars for the purpose of transporting drugs; and a couple who possessed British passports in the names of Terence William Abbot and Pauline Margaret Booth.

After telexing police in London and Washington through Interpol, the Italian investigators discovered that 'Terrence Abbott' was in fact the international acid-dealing fugitive, Ronald Stark, who had escaped the net of the US Federal Task Force when the Brotherhood of Eternal Love was rolled up in 1972. The photo on the British passport of Pauline Margaret Booth matched a photo ID of an American named Henrietta Ann Kaimer, who was Stark's wife.

Stark's safe deposit box in Rome was found to contain documents from his LSD laboratories in France and Belgium, including correspondence with members of the Brotherhood. There were also bottles of chemical substances, one of which was identified as synthetic psilocybin.

Stark went on trial in July 1976. Dramatically, he proclaimed himself to be a political prisoner and refused to recognise the court. He was found guilty and sentenced to fourteen years imprisonment for drug-smuggling plus a fine of $60,000. News of Stark's arrest and prosecution reached Detective Inspector Richard Lee, who had launched the Operation Julie investigation on 17 February 1976. Lee suspected that the British LSD ring headed by Richard Kemp was part of an international conspiracy of acid dealers which had continued the work of the Brotherhood of Eternal Love after it had been broken up by the US authorities in 1972. Lee wanted to go to Italy and interview Stark in prison but his request was turned down; and by the time (May 1977) the Italian authorities sent him the documents seized from Stark, the trial was over and Operation Julie was being been wound down. Some of the Stark documents did deal with his activities in the UK. There were letters from 1972, signed by Stark, from the 'Amalgamated Pharmaceutical Company' of Holland Rd London W14 ordering ergotamine tartrate from the West German company, Dr Rentschler. One letter discussed someone called 'David' and his connection with Amsterdam. Lee suspected that this might have been David Solomon, thus suggesting a link between Stark, Solomon and Sheni in Amsterdam as late as 1972 (Lee was sceptical of Richard Kemp's assurance that he had broken all contact with Stark in 1971). 'David', however, could also have been another American, David Linker, who was Stark's assistant.

Richard Lee had voiced suspicions that the LSD-producers had terrorist connections. Ronald Stark's fellow prisoners included a members of the terrorist Red Brigades. Unknown to Lee, in spring 1976, shortly before his trial, Stark made contact with the chief prosecutor of Pisa and passed on details of conversations he had had with Red Brigades leader, Renato Curcio. In July 1977, Stark complained to a Bologna prosecutor that information he had passed on had not led to arrests. Because of this failure, as he saw it, Stark stated that he had taken steps to provide *'certain people'* with information that would be enough to round up the Red Brigades leadership. The implication was that the 'certain people' were CIA.

In October 1978, Ronald Stark, having served over three years in prison, went to the Italian Court of Appeal and told the Judges, in Arabic, that he was really 'Khouri Ali' of a previously unheard of Palestinian commando organisation called 'Group 14'. In doing so, he was trying to convince his Red Brigades fellow prisoners and their supporters that he was a real revolutionary. But by the same token, Stark was trying to convince his police contacts that his 'Khouri Ali' guise was part of a CIA mission to infiltrate Middle Eastern terrorist groups. Italian police found correspondence in which he purported to be the business representative of Iman Moussa Al-Sadr. Summarising a report in *Panorama*, Lee and Shlain write in *Acid Dreams*:

> Stark's antics took him far afield. Occasionally he travelled to the Baalbek region of Lebanon, where he negotiated with a Shiite Muslim sect for shiploads of hashish. Stark claimed to be a business representative of Iman Moussa Sadr, a powerful Shiite warlord who controlled vast hashish plantations and a private army of 6,000 men. The

area under his dominion was said to include training camps used by the Palestinian Liberation Organization and other terrorist groups.

Iman Moussa Sadr was a powerful Shiite cleric. But he did not control vast hashish plantations, although no doubt some of his followers did and also led militias. So what was Stark doing in Lebanon? In August 1970, a plane loaded with Lebanese hash was forced to land in Crete where it was impounded by Greek police. Five Americans were arrested, including David Leigh Mantell, who was Nick Sand's LSD partner at the Cloverdale ranch in California. Stark's lawyer, Sam Goekjian, knew who to bribe in Greece and managed to get Mantell out of prison by the fall of 1971. As a pay-off Mantell introduced Ron Stark to the El-Masri family in Lebanon. As a result, according to Tim Scully,

> Ron's primary contact in Lebanon was the El-Masri family and he spent a fair amount of time visiting with them between 1972 and 1975. He was very interested in the more powerful THC derivatives such as the dimethylheptyl and he and his chemist (Tord Svenson) had decided by 1972 that the best raw material for making those derivatives was hash oil. I'm convinced that Ron's connection with the El-Masri family was motivated by his interest in making powerful THC derivatives and failing that in smuggling hash and/or hash oil for fun and profit and that any political connections were relatively incidental. Of course the Italians saw it differently

since they were seeing political conspiracies under every rock they turned over.

On 11 April 1979, following an appeal Stark lodged in Bologna, Judge Giorgio Floridia made the astonishing ruling that, 'an impressive series of scrupulously enumerated proofs' provided by Stark's defence team suggested that from 1960 onwards Stark 'belonged to the American secret services' and 'had entered the Middle East drug world in order to infiltrate armed organisations operating in that area and to gain contacts and information about European terrorist groups'. The judge noted that Stark couldn't be expected to say he was in the CIA because to do so on foreign soil would be a treasonable offense in the US. Floridia released Stark on bail, with the stipulation that he report to the Carabiniere twice a week. Days later, Stark checked into a Bologna cardiac surgery for 'acute myocardial infarction', a symptom of his old complaint, Reiters Syndrome. Then a telex arrived at Bologna Carabiniere HQ:

> A reliable confidential source has reported that Stark, according to what he had himself disclosed, was in a position to leave the country secretly with the assistance of American personnel. The localities indicated for his probable departure are Pisa or Vicenza.

Stark had flown. Judge Floridia's ruling elevated the Stark story to a new level of conspiracy theorising, drawing in parliamentarians as well as journalists. On June 4 1979, several weeks after Stark absconded, assistant prosecutor Claudio Nunziata, sent a 'contrary opinion' on the case to Judge

Floridia. Nunziata found that between February 1975, when Stark was incarcerated, and the appeal ruling of Autumn 1977 which reduced the sentence to 5 years, he had 'made every effort to become an infiltrator' of the Red Brigades, providing information to the counter terrorist officers of the Carabinieri. However, 'all of them, more or less, gave scarce importance to his information'. Information provided by Stark on the Red Brigades 'was defined as imaginative or already known and of public domain, or has never been verified'. The Carabiniere made it clear to Stark that in order to establish his effective capability as an infiltrator he would need to provide information regarding the location of Red Brigades suspects at large, such as safe-houses. But Stark did not provide any such information. Floridia's judgment had been based on 'proofs' consisting of documents provided by Stark, but Stark was greatly experienced in fooling authorities with false documentation.

Nunziata noted that after his appeal of autumn 1977 Stark had stopped supplying the Italian authorities with 'intelligence' gleaned from his fellow prisoners. From that point on Stark's concern was the prospect of being handed over to the American authorities as soon as he was released. Stark was now nourishing his longstanding contacts with American diplomats. Nunziata's report notes the 'very weird' friendly relations between Stark and a number of American diplomats, namely: Wendy Hansen, US vice-consul in Florence; Philip Taylor, US consul in Rome; and Charles Adams, an 'American diplomat'. Nunziata commented, it was 'not easy to understand also why the diplomats buzzed around Ron Stark', visiting him in Bologna prison on many occasions: 'It seems evident that the American officials nursed Ron Stark in order to receive information regarding the internal situation of the Italian prisons.'

After fleeing Italy in 1979, Stark disappeared from view. He surfaced again in 1982 when he was arrested in Holland for possession of 16 kilos of Lebanese hash plus some cocaine and heroin, and for illegal use of a radio transmitter. The Dutch authorities decided that, rather than put him on trial, it would be less trouble just to deport him. Stark was deported in 1983 to the US, where he was arrested on landing in New York to face the same Federal indictment from 1973 that sent Nick Sand and Tim Scully to the prison at McNeil Island (Sand, having been released on bail pending an appeal, fled to Canada and resumed acid manufacturing, while Scully opted to serve time and go straight). Stark was transferred to a prison in San Francisco as pre-trial proceedings got under way. From prison Stark acted as his own attorney, filing a motion for dismissal of the indictment on the grounds that the government had known exactly where he was when he was in Italian custody but had made no attempt to extradite him.

On December 8 1983, Joseph Russoniello, the Attorney General of Northern California, ruled that because of 'problems that have arisen in locating key witnesses abroad as well as important documentary evidence' the government could not proceed with a trial. The case was dismissed without prejudice and Stark walked free.

In 1984, when the Bologna prosecutor sought Stark's extradition to Italy, the US authorities sent a copy of his death certificate, dated 8 May 1984. This was greeted with some scepticism for the conspiracy theorists of the Italian press. But according to Tim Scully, whose source was someone close to Stark, who spoke to him on the telephone the day before he died, Stark was flying on cocaine and died the next day of a heart attack.

If CIA agents had at any point considered establishing a relationship with Stark – which might have been the case, considering his documented contacts with American diplomats – then it is likely that either he would have tried to con them just like he tried to con everyone else, or they would have realised he was too unreliable to be of any use to them. In Scully's assessment,

> Ron Stark was a very charming, playful, very intelligent pathological liar and con artist. He fooled me for many years. He presented himself to me as a sophisticated international businessman on the boards of directors of a number of large multinational corporations, a PhD biochemist and an MD medical doctor. He was none of those things but he could put up an amazingly good front.

16 – The Greening of Microdoctrine?

At 7a.m. on 25 March 1977, the Operation Julie police sledgehammered the doors and French windows of Henry Todd's house in Hampton Wick and discovered his LSD laboratory. Todd put on a brave face and asked them whether they had come to present him with the Queen's Award for Industry. It was graveyard humour with irony. The arrests that morning, of 130 people at 87 houses nationwide, could be compared with raiding a successful, though illicit, industry and arresting its production, supply and distribution teams. But it could also be compared with taking out the leadership of a political party or underground resistance organisation and all its regional organisers. Todd's erstwhile colleague, Richard Kemp, the unchallenged 'alchemist' of the British LSD Underground, certainly saw it in those terms:

> We have been hunted down, not because of a few bad trips or LSD-associated deaths, but because of the dramatic political effect we have been having.

After his arrest Richard Kemp was interviewed by Operation Julie executive commander, Detective Chief Superintendent Dennis Greenslade. The conversation revealed the gulf between two opposing views of reality and between two different times. Greenslade spoke like a colonial policeman trying to put a coolie opium pedlar in his place; Kemp responded like an arrogant intellectual having to endure an ignorant bureaucrat.

Kemp: You know nothing. You represent political repression.

Greenslade: It's all very well to assume that people have a wonderful time on your LSD. We have to clean up the mess. You have no appreciation of the amount of people all over the country having personal hallucinations.

Kemp: You know nothing.

Greenslade: I have travelled in the Far East and seen people on opium.

Kemp: The opiates are something else. Acid is different.

Greenslade: Whatever it is it is against the law.

Kemp: The law, and you, represent political repression.

When asked what he spent his money on, Kemp said he had supported rock festivals such as Windsor and Glastonbury, and had given money to Release, the organisation set up to help defendants in drugs cases. Kemp was asked if he had, 'supported politics,'

Kemp: Yes.

Greenslade: What organisations?'

Kemp: Head politics.

Greenslade: The names of the groups?

Kemp: I don't want to discuss it.

Kemp wrote an 8,000-word statement which he intended to present at Operation Julie trial, but was dissuaded from doing so by his lawyers who may have thought it was too political and insufficiently repentant. A week after he was sentenced to 14 years imprisonment parts of the document were printed in the *Cambrian News*, 17 March 1978. Patrick O'Brien, the journalist he passed the statement to, introduced it as 'Microdoctrine – the beliefs behind Kemp's LSD,' and summarised Kemp's views:

> In common with expert scientific opinion he was convinced that, if Earth's raw materials were to be conserved and pollution reduced to a tolerable level, there would be a revolution in people's attitude. And he believed LSD could spark changes in outlook and put the world on the road to survival.

In the document, Richard Kemp said,

> It has been my experience and that of many of those I know, that LSD helps to make one realise that happiness is a state of mind and not a state of ownership.

And,

> Insofar as LSD can catalyze such a change in members of the public, it can contribute to this end... I have never believed that LSD is the substitute for the hard work required to change oneself. One might say it is a signpost pointing a way to self-discovery.

Kemp insisted he was not advocating unrestricted use of the drug purely for hedonistic purposes:

> I would certainly support a system of social control, including education about the nature and use of LSD. Backed by laws, where appropriate, to protect those who are not fully able to take decisions for themselves... The present climate of opinion and law effectively forced me to make a choice between making LSD available without social controls, with the small risk inherent in this approach, or not making it available at all.

According to Leaf Fielding, whose politics might be best described as 'eco-anarchist':

> Something had seriously gone wrong with the human adventure. Unless we could sort it out we were for the chop. Protesting about the bad state of affairs had little effect. People had to see for themselves what was going on. With acid there was a good chance that they would. I had, and I wasn't alone. In the summer of '67 hundreds of thousands of high-spirited trippers were optimistic that mankind was on the point of taking the next step up the evolutionary ladder. The qualities that had enabled homo sapiens to manipulate his environment had also placed him on the brink of destruction... LSD was the tool that could help us to see a way back from the brink, by enabling us to appreciate that fundamentally we are all one – while giving us the confidence to celebrate our

diversity and our differences. What fun, having a mission to save the world.

The fun, as we have seen, had its dark side. Christine Bott's later reflections expressed a certain disillusion regarding the 'mission':

> The original idealist group fired by a vision of global social change had changed itself into a more mundane, more criminal gang. And I too had lost the inner certainty of being on a mission of doing the right thing at the right historical moment that would nudge the world into waking up and seeing where we were clearly headed. I believed that the process of industrialisation, culminating in the release of atomic energy, was an opening up of knowledge that was beyond our moral and spiritual level of development to control. With the right preparation, mind set, setting and guide, an LSD trip can carry an individual into a brief experience of cosmic oneness such as had previously occurred spontaneously to a very few, as was the goal of mystics of all faiths and of people who maintained the knowledge and use of their aboriginal and sacred rights. I was far removed from the street reality that was the destination of most of our acid, and I didn't want to know or look too closely at the possibility that flooding the unprepared nervous system with such as overwhelming blast of energy could leave individuals in a burnt-out condition.

In the British LSD 'business model', radical idealism constantly found itself at the mercy of the pragmatic realism demanded by capitalism. Nonetheless the ideas of some, if not all, of the acid heads represented the growing concerns about war, erosion of the biosphere, and other threats to the future of humanity. Beginning with Rachel Carson's book of 1962, *Silent Spring*, which documented the uncontrolled effects of pesticides and pollutants on the environment, these ideas increasingly took hold through the 1970s and '80s.

Christine Bott's writings suggest that had she not fallen into criminality and subsequent imprisonment, she might have become a very effective environmental campaigner or public health advocate, if not a feminist politician. Bott, corresponded from prison with Robert Demarest, a librarian and researcher in Florida.

Bott's prison reading, which Demarest sent her, reflected her continued interest in ecological and 'alternative health' issues: *Journal of the American Institute of Homeopathy*; Gary Snyder's book, *The Real Work*; Stewart Brand's *Whole Earth Catalogue*; *Resurgence* magazine, *Evolution Quarterly*, etc. Bott planned to write an account of the years she had spent in prison and asked Demarest to send her William Strunk's *The Elements of Style*. Commenting on Inspector Richard Lee's book, she wrote:

> Whilst there were some blatant distortions and inventions, it seemed to me a reasonable account from the police viewpoint, even revealing something of their schizophrenic state of mind when the brain

damaged fiends they had chased for so long turned out to be nice people who didn't behave as criminals were supposed to do... surprise, surprise!

Christine Bott died in 2007. In 2021, her memoir of her LSD 'caper' was finally published, with an introduction by her close friend, Catherine Hayes.

*

Like atomic power and artificial intelligence, LSD was discovered in the closing years of World War Two. Since then, atomic bombs and computers have been the constant source of fears that combined they might bring about the destruction of humanity. LSD has aroused similar fears. Albert Hofmann, the Swiss chemist who discovered its effects in 1943, likened the LSD trip to an 'inner bomb'. He warned that, if improperly used and distributed, LSD might bring about more destruction than an atomic detonation. But it has also been argued that, if *properly* used and distributed, LSD use might actually change people's consciousness for the better and help to prevent nuclear war – and environmental catastrophe.

Professor David Nutt, who sat on the British Labour government's Advisory Committee on the Misuse of Drugs until he was sacked in 2009, argues that the study of psychedelics is essential for understanding the nature of consciousness itself:

> This is core neuroscience. This is about humanity at its deepest level. It is fundamental to understanding ourselves. And the only way to study consciousness is to change it. Psychedelics change consciousness

in a way that is unique, powerful, and perpetual – of course we have to study them.

Denying or ignoring the science on the grounds that it 'sends the wrong message' is equivalent to protecting planet-burning jobs and businesses by denying or ignoring the prospect of ecological catastrophe. Denying or ignoring the science on the grounds that it 'sends the wrong message', is equivalent as denying the possibility of ecological catastrophe to protect planet-burning jobs and businesses. Whatever the 'message' of the defendants in the Operation Julie trial, it wasn't taken up by the mainstream media. John May, reporting in the *New Musical Express* expressed one of the few dissenting opinions:

> Perhaps the saddest aspect of the whole affair is the lack of support and interest from the 'hip' or head community... But a few short years ago Kemp and Co would have been hailed as 'psychedelic outlaws'.' Now it seems most people are content to accept the official word on the subject and go back to their Bovril and bedroom slippers. On the other hand, many people I spoke to were beside themselves with anger at the whitewash job performed on the affair.

Finally, in considering the impact the availability of LSD had on the 'culture', we may quote David Solomon. Remanded in prison before the trial, he wrote to his friend Lee Harris, editor of *Home Grown* magazine, suggesting that it was time for the LSD counterculture to treat the Julie defendants as political prisoners facing a show trial:

> It seems morally unthinkable that famous pop artists and groups—who owe much to Alice – would not cough up. Everyone from Bob Dylan to the Stones, Lennon, McCartney et alia infinitum should be asked for sizeable contributions to help pay for our immense legal bill and keep our families fed and housed.

Those who owed so much to 'Alice' were lauded with acclaim, fortune and fame; those who provided it were landed with prison, poverty and notoriety. In any case the solidarity was not forthcoming. But if anything Solomon was understating his case. As we have seen, the British Acid Underground was characterised by talent, idealism and courage, as well as greed, cynicism and treachery. The same thing could be said, however, of the entire acid-fuelled sub-culture that impacted on the social totality; not just in music, but also in the visual arts, literature, religion, philosophy, and the sciences – and did so for the better.

EXTRA – LSD-IRA?
David Solomon, James Joseph McCann and Operation Julie

1 – *An Island Mystery*

Stephen Bentley, in his book, *Undercover: Operation Julie - The Inside Story*, writes of his role in the elite police squad that targeted British LSD production and distribution networks; culminating in 1977 with 'the biggest drugs bust in history'. In 2016, a reader of Bentley's blog wrote to him about an encounter in 1972 between his late father and leading LSD conspirator, David Solomon, who six years later got a ten-year prison sentence in the 1978 'Julie' trial. Bentley's anonymous reader said that when his father put his house in Anglesey up for sale, Solomon turned up as a potential buyer. Solomon, with his public face of a successful American author and journalist, also introduced the reader's father to Richard Kemp, who was secretly the chief chemist of the LSD ring, and his partner, Christine Bott, a medical doctor. Bentley says that although his reader was a child at the time he 'distinctly recalled' that Solomon was accompanied on occasion by an Irishman, who later turned out to be James McCann, 'IRA volunteer'. The reader 'described and witnessed this volunteer as "going mental" at his father... Solomon calmed the Irishman down and they left'. Bentley writes:

> David Solomon, for me, was always a dark character. I always felt there was something sinister about him... He had approached [Richard] Kemp to manufacture both LSD and a synthesised form of cannabis. It turns out he was also associated with IRA terrorists. He also had links to other terrorists. These links were never followed up.

This is unprecedented. No previous account has claimed that in 1972 Solomon and McCann were conspiring together in Anglesey, or that the British LSD Underground (AKA the Microdot Gang) made any kind of link with the Irish Republican Army. In my previous book, *Psychedelic Tricksters*, I noted that the description in Bentley's book of McCann 'going mental' at someone for no apparent reason would not surprise those who knew him, such as his partner in hash-smuggling, Howard Marks. However, it seemed evident that whatever interests David Solomon and James McCann had in common, LSD wouldn't have been one of them, since as far as it is known McCann was never interested in it, either for personal use or commercial gain. They did, however, have some interests in common, not least smuggling shipments of cannabis – and more, as we shall see. My attitude then was sceptical, if not entirely dismissive.

In June 2020, Bentley's correspondent wrote to me from Anglesey. He is Harvey Mason, son of the late John and Cynthia Mason. Harvey told me he thought Bentley's interpretation of their correspondence was not entirely accurate. As regards McCann 'going mental' at his father:

At that time in 1972 I was 4 years old. I only have vague recollections of things that happened like my father fixing a broken table the following morning and not understanding why he was angry. Other than that, it's what my parents have told me about the events that transpired. James McCann did not visit the house. Solomon did...

Harvey went on to tell me that Bentley's account of the affair was by no means the whole story. Harvey sent me copies of contemporaneous notes he had taken of his parents' recollections, plus various relevant documents he had inherited. Harvey's father believed he had been 'subject to a dirty tricks campaign to keep him quiet'. Harvey, convinced that there was more to be discovered, suggested that I might like to dig into it. He was also keen to do some digging himself.

2 – *Smugglers Creek*

John Mason was a civil engineer who worked on several construction projects, including some for the nuclear and defence industries. His family home, *Saith Mor,* was an old cottage in Amlwch, on the northern coast of the island of Anglesey. It had a small chalet attached, which could be rented out. The property went all the way down to the shore, and a path led to a secluded creek, which would, Harvey says, have been 'perfect for smuggling'. The Masons also ran a small restaurant, named the *Seven Seas,* on Mona Street, Amlwch. A few doors down the street stood a jewellery workshop owned by one Derek Francis Donovan. When the Masons decided to sell Saith Mor, Donovan offered to find a buyer in return for a commission on the sale. It was Derek Donovan who introduced David Solomon to John Mason.

During his visit to Amlwch, Solomon stayed for a few nights at the Bull Bay Hotel and visited the Masons' restaurant several times. Mason took Solomon on a crabbing expedition along the coast. In conversation, Mason recalled, Solomon talked about the pleasures of taking certain drugs and hinted, half-jokingly, that he was or had been connected to the CIA (in World War Two he had served in military intelligence). Mason also recalled that Solomon 'became nervy' when someone present casually mentioned that Mason was friendly with the local police: he had been reporting suspicious night-time activities at Bull Bay, such as lights flashing on and off at sea, and boats loading and unloading.

Richard Kemp and Christine Bott turned up at Saith Mor along with Gerald Lyn Thomas, an American chemical engineer. They presented themselves to John Mason as working for Thomas' company, 'Pollution Control Associates' and left a business card. After viewing the house, Kemp, Bott and Thomas headed off to Trearddur Bay, to look at other properties on the island. Solomon left Amlwch without clinching a deal to buy the Masons' property. On 8 June 1972, Solomon wrote a friendly, apologetic letter to John Mason to say the deal was off:

> Just a note in line with my promise to get in touch with you as soon as I could gather my 'clan' together for a group decision regarding your house and property. I deeply regret that I was unable to get my people together on this... to swing all the

money... I have been in many parts of this world and have known people both high and low: you are an original and I do not rate you below any man I have ever met. So I do hope that my inability to swing this thing does not alter my having found a friend, a fellow poacher of the wilds of the universe.

The Masons never heard from any of them again. Kemp and Bott were travelling around in a caravan at the time. Later, with financial help from others in the Microdot Gang, they bought a house near Tregaron, Ceredigion, to live in. With another American, Paul Arnaboldi, they bought an old mansion at Plas Llysyn, near Carno, to house their laboratory.

Mason's house in Amlwch, following Solomon's withdrawal, was bought by Derek Donovan, who moved in with his family. The Masons moved to a smaller property, having also sold their restaurant. The meeting in 1972 with David Solomon, however, would come back to haunt them.

3 – *Operation Julie*

In March 1977, five years after meeting Solomon, John Mason read the press coverage of the Operation Julie arrests. He immediately recognised the names of some of the defendants and contacted the police to tell them what he knew. As well as Solomon's letter, Mason showed the police the business card Gerald Thomas had given him: 'Pollution Control Associates: Water Pollution Specialists, BCM Pulocon, WCI V6XX. Tel 01 405 0463/4.' The company turned out to have been largely a front for Thomas's endeavours with Solomon to make synthetic cocaine and THC in a laboratory.

Neither Mason's statement to the police on meeting with Solomon and friends nor the business card figured at the Operation Julie trial, which was held in early 1978. But the reference to 'water pollution' may well have been the basis for an allegation that the defendants had seriously planned to pollute the water supply with LSD. Days after the trial ended, the *Mirror*, on 9 March 1978, ran a front-page story which claimed,

> Top chemist Richard Kemp and his mistress... planned to blow a million minds simultaneously by pouring pure LSD into the reservoirs serving Birmingham. Detectives were horrified when they heard what the drug barons had in mind.

The story, which was police-sourced, was written by Ed Laxton, the ghost writer for Operation Julie undercover officer Martyn Pritchard's book, *Busted! The Sensational Life-Story of an Undercover Hippie* (1978). The prosecutors in the trial had known better than to run the 'acid in the water supply' allegation past a jury; if they had the defence would simply have got a qualified scientist to testify that LSD would have been quite ineffective in a reservoir because dilution and the chlorine content would have neutralised it. The *Mirror* story was obviously intended to quell any sympathy the public might have had for the hippie defendants.

If the police did make use of the business card for such 'PR' purposes, they didn't pay much attention to Mason's most startling contention: that he hadn't just met the Operation Julie defendants, but also an Irishman the police now knew as James Joseph McCann, IRA associate and fugitive. Cynthia Mason told the police that Solomon, as well as visiting the house, dined at the *Seven Seas* accompanied by the Irishman; twice when she was serving and the last time when John Mason was front of house. After the incident of the Irishman 'going mental' at John Mason, Solomon returned to the restaurant to say it had been a case of mistaken identity.

Several months earlier, in 1971, James McCann escaped from Crumlin Road Prison in Belfast and fled to the Irish Republic, after which his whereabouts remained unknown for six years. But at the very time the Masons were talking to the police, McCann shot back into the news, this time with his face in an accompanying photograph. He had been arrested in Canada in July 1977 and deported. He landed in France, where he was arrested at the request of the West German police to face extradition for his alleged part in the bombing of a British Army base in 1973. The French court rejected the extradition application on the grounds that the alleged offence was political. But the French authorities wanted McCann off their hands and deported him to Ireland, where he once again disappeared.

The Masons identified McCann from photographs shown them by the police. As McCann was still at large, they feared for their safety because they believed they had witnessed a connection between the LSD conspiracy and Irish republican terrorism. The only other witness was Derek Donovan, who had introduced Solomon to John Mason. Yet, as far as the police were concerned, he did not appear to figure in the Julie investigation. John Mason wondered why.

4 – Derek Donovan

Derek Francis Donovan (1934-2007) was born in Tooting, south London. Like many growing up in the poorer parts of London during World War Two, Donovan was drawn into petty crime. By his early teens, he was making a name for himself as a snooker player in the local halls and mixing with other young delinquents, including Charles and Eddie Richardson from nearby Camberwell. Destined for later notoriety as celebrity gangsters, the Richardsons were already building their scrap metal empire from the ruins of the London Blitz. In the immediate post-war years, Donovan, like Charles Richardson, did time in reform schools and then the armed forces. But unlike Richardson, who feigned madness to get a discharge from the army, Donovan served for twelve years in the Royal Air Force, specialising in developing new technology, such as flight simulation. Military discipline did not, however, 'straighten' him out. In 1959, when serving as an RAF Corporal at St Athans, he was prosecuted for stealing cigarettes from a vending machine by inserting metal disks he made in an RAF workshop. For this he got a three-month prison sentence, reduced on appeal to a fine. In January 1960, Donovan was committed for trial to Glamorgan Quarter Sessions on charges of stealing equipment from the Air Ministry, worth about £200, to sell to a scrap dealer.

Although there is no evidence that Donovan ever did business with the Richardsons, he was selling stolen RAF material as scrap during the period the Richardsons were buying it. Charlie Richardson claimed that the Metropolitan police were hounding him because he couldn't bribe enough of them with a cut of the profits he was making from stolen scrap metal. Richardson escaped prosecution by bribing witnesses and donating to the 'police fund'. Derek Donovan, in contrast, was investigated by the RAF Special Investigations Branch which, compared to the Met, was regarded as corruption-free. Donovan pleaded not guilty but was convicted and given a six months prison sentence. Surprisingly, Donovan's imprisonment did not end his RAF career, which lasted a couple of more years and saw him promoted to the rank of sergeant.

Donovan served part of his time in Kenya. There, he met his future wife, Terry, who was from the mid-Wales town of Llanidloes. After leaving the RAF, Derek and Terry moved to Amlwch, Anglesey, where he opened a workshop and put his metal-working skills to good use as a jeweller, clock repairer and occasional gunsmith. In the mid-1960s he served as an Amlwch town councillor. After the Language Act of 1967 ended the ban on using Welsh in public administration Donovan found himself at a loss for words at council meetings. His complaints about this were ignored by the British media but the story travelled to the USA (which Donovan never visited) and the *Boston Globe* of May 9 1967 reported, with tongue-in-cheek, that Donovan, an Englishman with an Irish name, was demanding to have a translator on hand at Welsh council meetings.

As a jeweller Donovan made regular trips to London's Hatton Garden, for meetings with dealers in side-streets to exchange envelopes of cash for pouches of diamonds. He also made jewellery from tourmaline, which he imported from Nigeria. Tourmaline, a crystalline boron silicate, is believed to have magical powers guarding against 'negative thought patterns'. This may well have been of interest to Terry Donovan who was a dabbler in the occult – an interest not shared by Derek. Terry was a practicing witch and avid reader of the books of Aleister Crowley, the notorious English magician. Terry socialised with a community of hippies at Mynydd Mellech, which is near Amlwch. In the early 1970s there was a hippy commune in the area (at Ynys Mon) which spawned the punk bands Aslan and the Ruts. The 'pagan'/hippie aspect offers another possible connection between Solomon and Donovan. The author, George Andrews, who collaborated with Solomon on the 1973 anthology, *Drugs and Sexuality*, also edited an anthology entitled *Drugs and Magic* in 1975. Andrews is also known to have been one of Solomon's LSD distributors, although he was never arrested for it.

Apart from working as a jeweller Donovan had an important source of income in property, using the technique of 'flipping', i.e. making a profit by taking possession of a house before actually paying for it, if ever. In the mid-1970s he took over the Grenville Hotel on Mona Street, Almwch and made money out it for some time without paying the seller. Donovan managed to get an alcohol licence for a bar in adjoining premises, which was frequented by welders from Liverpool who were building an oil pipeline. The liberties Donovan was taking with other people's property may have had awkward consequences: a regular at the Grenville recalled that one day a stranger walked in and asked, 'Who owns this bar?' On being told that Derek Donovan owned it but wasn't around, the stranger said, 'Well, we need to talk', and walked out. One of the Liverpudlians exclaimed 'Fuck me, do you know who that is?' He had recognized the stranger as an associate of Dougie Flood, property magnate and leading figure of the Manchester Quality Street Gang. Peter Walsh, in his book *Drug War*, records that certain high-ranking police officers in the Greater Manchester Police stated that 'The Quality Street Gang is the name given to a group of criminals who are... the organisers of incidents of major crime in the city.'

In April 1980, a boat named the *Eloise* was seized in south Anglesey near Newborough, loaded with one and a half tons of cannabis. The boat had been tracked from the Mediterranean by a multi-agency taskforce, codenamed 'Yashmak'. The lead agency in this operation was the British Customs special investigations unit, Alpha. The cannabis scam had been masterminded by Arend der Horst, a 'Mr Big' of hash-smuggling, who remained in the Netherlands, safe from extradition. Horst was a one-time associate of Howard Marks, as was Charles Radcliffe, who supervised the Anglesey shipment from his farmhouse in Devon. The boat crew and a landing party who were waiting on the beach were all arrested. Several others were arrested elsewhere, including Radcliffe. At a trial the following year, nine of those arrested got a total of 22 years imprisonment. One of the boat crew was Anglesey resident, Allan Stephen Lloyd (35), a professional yachtsman, of Tynn Llwyn, Liangristiolus. Lloyd, who had chosen the spot for the landing, got a two year sentence. There is no evidence that Stephen Lloyd knew Derek Donovan, but it is known that Donovan was one of several men in Anglesey who were suspected of involvement in the scam but never charged. Donovan's home and premises were raided and searched for four days. He claimed he had been raided because of a dispute with the tax authorities over his VAT bill (the Yashmak investigation was after all led by HM Revenue and Customs). He also claimed that the previous owner of his house had been a drug dealer. But as the previous owner had been John Mason, this couldn't have been true. When Donovan moved out of the house after his business went bankrupt in the mid-1980s, a hand grenade was discovered by the new owners during renovation. The grenade was blown up on the beach by the bomb disposal squad. Donovan claimed the house had been owned in 1950s by a retired army officer; hence the presence of the grenade. But given that the house had been completely renovated by John Mason during his ownership, this seemed questionable.

According to a source close to Donovan, he used to receive regular visits from a 'lady from MI5'. When asked to expand further on this claim, the source backed off; refusing to confirm or deny and declining to comment further. The most that can be said of this is that there is no reason to think the source wasn't telling the truth about what Donovan had said – which is not to say that Donovan *was* telling the truth.

5 – *James McCann, David Solomon, Howard Marks and Frendz*

Like Derek Francis Donovan, James Joseph McCann had an interest in jewellery. According to David Leigh's book, *High Times: the Life and Times of Howard Marks*, 'There is some concrete evidence that he [McCann] spent a period in Amsterdam selling stolen jewellery.' McCann also claimed to have been associated with the Richardson gang. McCann is also known to have worked as an enforcer for the property gangster, Nicholas Hoogstraten.

In London in February 1971, McCann gate-crashed an editorial meeting of a left-wing underground magazine called *Friends* – later renamed *Frendz* – and to impress them, showed off a sawn-off shotgun he pulled from inside his coat – a stunt he had perfected during his time as an enforcer. McCann told the hippie journalists that he was part of a movement called 'Free Belfast', which he claimed represented a growing anarchist/hippie tendency within the Six Counties. McCann organised a trip to Belfast for a group of *Friends* staff and other alternative press people. In late March 1971, McCann was holding court with former *International Times* editor Felix de Mendelssohn, American photographer Joe Stevens and Irish journalist Pete McCartan in the common room of Belfast Queen's University. To everyone's horror, McCann suddenly pulled a sawn-off shotgun and threw a Molotov cocktail into the yard. This led to a chase by a plain-clothes patrol of the Royal Ulster Constabulary followed by an armed stand-off. McCann surrendered and the four of them were arrested and remanded to Crumlin Road gaol. Jill Marcuson, wife of *Friends* editor, Alan Marcuson, and other anarchists present in Belfast were also arrested.

Alan Marcuson, who edited *Friends* for 28 issues, from 1969-71, says that for him and Jill their involvement ended that day, 'when everyone was in Belfast'. He had an appointment to meet John Lennon in Apple's offices to ask for finance for *Friends*, but en route he passed a newspaper headline which said 'Ten in Anarchist Bomb Gang': 'It was Felix and Jim McCann, Jilly and Joe Stevens. And I walked into this meeting white as a sheet. I didn't get as far as asking him for money.'

McCann managed to break out of the prison by sawing through the cell bars (how he got the saw is mystery). He referred to himself from then on as the 'shamrock pimpernel'. McCann was not in the strict sense an 'IRA Volunteer', i.e. a sworn-in member. But according to a Wikipedia entry, in the late 1960s and early 1970s McCann was close to the Provisional IRA in Belfast and smuggled shipments of weapons through the port of Greenore in Ireland.

McCann's encounter with *Friends* magazine led to editors Alan Marcuson and Charles Radcliffe introducing him to their hash-smuggling associates, Howard Marks and Graham Plinston. Once McCann was free and in the Irish Republic he was back in business. With Marks and Plinson, McCann, using his

Republican contacts at Shannon Airport, formed a syndicate for flying in Afghan and Nepalese hash.

As a writer and researcher on drug-use, Solomon cultivated links with several London underground journals – *Friends* included. Steve Abrams (whose dealings with David Solomon and his fellow American LSD conspirator, Ronald Stark, are described elsewhere in this book) told me of a conversation he had in 1971 with Bernie Simons, the London solicitor representing the the members of the *Friends* delegation who were arrested in Belfast. Simons (who also represented Howard Marks) said that, over lunch at the Oxford and Cambridge Club, Stark had offered to help out the Belfast defendants' case financially (though this never came to anything) and 'took some interest in McCann'. At this time Solomon was distributing the LSD made in Stark's Paris laboratory; so he too may have taken 'some interest' in McCann. Solomon had been responsible for getting Richard Kemp to work for Stark in his Paris laboratory to make LSD.

By the end of 1971, the Kemp-Stark relationship had ended and Solomon's relationship with Stark had cooled. Solomon, however, had procured enough ergotamine tartrate to set up his own LSD production venture. As he needed a chemist, he turned to Dick Pountain, chemist for the lobbying group, SOMA (Society of Mental Awareness) and writer for *Friends*. Pountain, in correspondence with me, confirms: 'I was indeed approached by Solomon to work for Julie, but I declined his kind offer once I recognised him as a foul-tempered sociopath - a couple of rungs below MacCann on the ladder.' Pountain only met McCann once, 'enough to recognise him as a psychopath and avoid future contact'. Pountain never met Stark, but recalls that Alan Marcuson did meet Stark once. Marcuson also knew McCann and Solomon, though in the latter case, according to Pountain, 'not very well'. Pountain thinks it doubtful that Alan Marcuson introduced Solomon to McCann, who was at the time hiding out in the Irish Republic. On the other hand he doesn't say he couldn't have. Certainly, Marcuson knew of McCann's location in the Irish Republic (Marcuson did not respond to enquiries on that matter). Pountain adds that given the 'underground' was such a 'small world' Solomon and McCann *could* have met 'a dozen different ways'.

Charles Radcliffe, for his part, did not last long in the new Marks-McCann setup. When, in late-1972, Radcliffe complained to Howard Marks that he was owed money for his 'research' role for the Shannon Airport scam, McCann telephoned Radcliffe and threatened to kill his family if he persisted in the claim. That was last time he heard from McCann and was the end of his collaboration with Marks, who had given McCann Radcliffe's telephone number.

6 – MI6

The writers for *Friends/Frendz* magazine, as well as James McCann and Howard Marks, were all on the radar of the security services. A retired police Special Branch officer who worked in Northern Ireland and Britain in the 1970s said that he knew 'quite a lot about *Friends*', because '*Friends* was infiltrated big style'. He said that it wasn't Special Branch that monitored the magazine but the security services, who passed on to the Branch a lot of 'verifications'; for 'propaganda to be honest'. Without naming anyone, he said that a lot of people associated with the magazine were 'compromised'. He added that McCann wasn't the only person connected with *Friends* magazine who would have been of interest, because part of the remit was to investigate 'associated links' between republican terrorism in Ireland and 'other' (unspecified) terrorist organisations: 'They [Friends] were infiltrated for whatever reason and information about the IRA was part of the intelligence chain that ended up with us.'

After Howard Marks and co met James McCann through contacts at *Friends* the relationship attracted the attention of the security services. According to Marks' autobiography, *Mr Nice*, in late 1972 he was approached by Hamilton McMillan, an old chum from Oxford who was now working for MI6. McMillan wanted to use Marks' Amsterdam dress shop, 'Annabelinda', as a front for MI6's monitoring of IRA activity. Marks agreed to work for MI6, but claims in *Mr Nice* that when he learned the immediate target was McCann, he decided to play a double game. Marks warned McCann that MI6 had him under surveillance and therefore probably knew about his smuggling operation at Shannon Airport.

Although it was late-1972 when Marks was recruited by MI6, the agency would have seen reports from Dutch intelligence as far back as early 1971 about Marks and his colleague Plinston linking up with McCann; and would have known that in October 1971 'Dutch' Doherty of the Belfast IRA was arrested and found to have Marks' name and former address in Britain in his contact list. Doherty had been given Marks' details by McCann. The reports reached the security services but were concealed from both the Metropolitan Police Central Drugs Intelligence Unit and British Customs.

One obvious reason to discount John Mason's testimony that he saw McCann in Wales in 1972 would be the unlikelihood of a wanted terrorist chancing a trip across the Irish Sea. However, according to Peter Walsh's book, *Drug War*, McCann's shipments of Afghan hash at Shannon Airport 'were then subdivided and ferried in cars to the UK'. McCann was certainly reckless enough to come to Britain, possibly on a clandestine landing by boat (in the early 1970s Irish fishing boats were using ports in Anglesey). As McCann boasted to Howard Marks, 'Fuck the Welsh ferry. And no fucker searches the kid. If the boys can take guns over every day for the struggle, and farmers can take their pigs over for bigger subsidies, I'm fucking sure I can take over some fucking bananas.' One thing he wouldn't have known was that had he made the trip and been checked by police or customs he wouldn't have been arrested because MI6 wanted both him and Marks left alone. Peter Walsh in *Drug War* quotes an officer of HM Custom's Special Investigations branch, Alpha, saying that, as regards Marks, 'we had a good idea where he was but we weren't allowed to touch him'. The same must have applied to McCann.

1972 was a bad year for MI6 in Ireland. In 1972, MI6 was recruiting and running agents in the Irish Republic. Two of them, former British soldier Kenneth Littlejohn and his brother Keith, carried out a number of bank robberies which were then falsely attributed to the Official IRA. On 12 October 1972, they were caught after an armed robbery of a bank in Dublin. This led to their outing by the Irish press as MI6 assets. In the same period MI6 was exposed for running an agent inside the Gardai Special Branch after he was arrested in Dublin for passing on top-secret files to MI6. These scandals were exposed at the very time MI6 was monitoring Howard Marks and James McCann.

In November 1973, Marks was arrested by the Dutch police for his part in smuggling cannabis to the US hidden in loud speakers for rock concerts. Shortly before this, according to MI6, the agency had severed contact with him. Either MI6 strongly suspected or knew that Marks was double-crossing, or wanted to avoid further exposure of the agency's collaboration with criminals – or both (according to Charles Radcliffe, Marks told him and several other dope-smugglers that he was playing the 'great game' with MI6 as a double agent). Marks jumped bail in Amsterdam, went underground and resumed smuggling. The Marks-MI6 affair was finally exposed in July 1979, when the *New Statesman* published a leaked police report.

A month after the leaking of the report, McCann was arrested by the Gardai in Naas, County Kildare for his role in a 850 pound shipment of marijuana from Thailand. McCann's cannabis-smuggling apparently embarrassed and angered the IRA; he was reportedly beaten up in jail whilst on remand. At the trial he claimed he had been set up by a British intelligence plot involving the drug-dealer and MI6 agent, Howard Marks. As the Marks-MI6 connection had been confirmed in the public domain, the trial judge directed the jury to acquit McCann.

In between McCann's arrest and subsequent acquittal, Marks was himself arrested. On the night of December 29 1979, the tugboat 'Karob' deposited 15 tons of Columbian dope on Scotland's West Coast. The arrangements were made by Marks' American contacts in the US Brotherhood of Eternal Love. According to Marks' accomplice, Patrick Lane, a detachment of rogue US Marines assisted the landing. The *Karob* was previously owned by the Anglesey salvaging company, Holyhead Towing, under the name *Afon Wen*. The crew were never identified. The inland distribution of the cannabis was, however, penetrated by British Customs investigators, who discovered Marks' role in the scam and arrested him. Marks admitted to doing the accounts for the operation, but claimed at his trial that he had been acting on behalf of MI6 to see if McCann was behind it. A Mexican intelligence officer appeared for the defence and claimed that Mark's had been providing intelligence on right-wing narco-terrorists. The prosecution couldn't prove that the Mexican wasn't telling the truth, or that he was being bribed (which he was). After the prosecution conceded that MI6 had indeed recruited him, Marks was acquitted by the jury. Once again MI6, the Secret Intelligence Service, was left facing embarrassing questions (which it never answered) about its illegal actions. There was then, as evidenced above, much going on in 1972 that the security services might have feared exposure of several years later when John Mason began asking the police awkward questions.

7 – *Blacklisting*

In 1980 John Mason applied for a job as a joiner at Sellafield nuclear power plant with the Balfour Beatty construction company. Balfour wrote to tell him that his application had been accepted and he should report for work on 6 October 1980. Then days after he received the letter Balfour Beatty notified him that the job offer had been withdrawn. No explanation was given. Working at Sellafield would have required a security clearance; the most likely explanation for rejecting Mason would have been that he failed it.

Mason began to suspect that he might be on some sort of MOD/Police database/blacklist for MOD work. Although it wasn't public knowledge at the time, the Balfour Beatty company was one of the largest subscribers to the blacklisting services of the Economic League which, with the assistance of police Special Branch, accumulated files on around 22,000 people. Names were entered into the files on the basis of trade union activities, political views or just a reputation for 'causing trouble'.

John Mason was no trade-union stalwart. In 1979, during the 'winter of discontent', Mason had travelled to Spennymoor, County Durham for his mother's funeral, only to find that the council gravediggers were on strike. He and his brother dug the grave themselves, and were featured doing so on BBC television news. Technically he was strike-breaking; but he was also a 'trouble maker' in the sense that he was not prepared to let anyone stop him from exercising his right, as he saw it, to give his mother a proper burial.

In 1982 to '83, John Mason tried to get the press to address his concerns that his difficulties in finding employment might be linked to a cover-up regarding Solomon, McCann and Donovan. According to Cynthia Mason's recollection, he was in contact with the *Mail on Sunday* and the *Observer*. But just before Mason was due to give an interview, police officers sent up from Staffordshire to Scotland walked onto the building site where he was working and pulled him in for questioning about the murder of 11-year-old Susan Maxwell. The body of the girl, who was abducted in Cornhill-on-Tweed, was found on 12 August 1982 near Uttoxeter, 264 miles away her home. Mason, exposed to his workmates as a suspect in a horrendous child-murder case, had to leave his job and return home to north Wales, where he had a nervous breakdown. Harvey Mason recalls:

> He wasn't even allowed to get his time sheets to prove his he was on the site. Someone had deliberately told the workforce he had been arrested for the murder and he came within a hair's breadth of a beating. He left the site, and had what can only be described as a nervous breakdown. I remember the time well. I was sent by my mother to get our local doctor at his home just around the corner. Eventually the police said he was no longer of interest.

In late 1983 John Mason, out the blue, was offered a job in Saudi Arabia by a Saudi company called KAL Enterprises which had an office in London. The owner, Saleh Abdullah Kamel, was a leading Saudi royal and businessman, likely to have been on friendly terms with MI6 which, after all, was the foreign intelligence service of a strategic ally of the Saudi regime. Mason took the job, which involved digging wells and irrigation, and flying around the Middle-East in a rickety World War Two Dakota in the company of an ex-South African mercenary. The work was very well paid, but Mason couldn't help suspecting that someone had pulled strings with the Saudis just to get him out of the way.

In 1985, Mason finally got confirmation from the police that he was no longer 'of interest' in the investigation of Susan Maxwell's murder (five years later the actual culprit, Robert Black, was caught and convicted of raping and murdering four girls aged between 5 and 11 in the years 1981 to 1986).

Mason suspected that his wrongful arrest for murder might have been linked to the apparent black-listing and to a cover-up regarding Solomon, McCann and Donovan. In 1985 he contacted Chester Stern, the chief crime correspondent at the *Mail on Sunday.* That same year Mason was granted a meeting with Sir Philip Myers, former Chief Constable of North Wales, now Her Majesty's Chief Inspector of Constabulary. Myers – who Mason found to be 'a real gentleman' – agreed to do some digging as to why the Staffordshire Police (who had found Susan Maxwell's body) had gone to make the arrest in Scotland. Myers told Mason, 'All I can tell you is the intelligence that led to your arrest came from the London Metropolitan Police.' Myers, however, did not or would not divulge who in the London Met was responsible for putting Mason in the frame.

Sir Philip Myers was by means innocent of covering up 'sensitive' security matters. John Stalker, Deputy Chief Constable of Greater Manchester, was sent to Belfast in 1983 to investigate the allegations of a police shoot-to-kill policy and collusion with Loyalist paramilitaries engaged in the murder of republican 'targets'. In 1986, just as he was due to present a final report, which recommended the prosecution of several RUC officers, he was accused of having criminal associations with the Manchester Quality Street Gang. Stalker was later cleared of the allegations, by which time his report had been buried. Asked years later as to who had been responsible for his downfall, Stalker said, 'I believe that essentially it was Sir Philip Myers. He was the prime mover, with various unknown people from the Northern Ireland Office with the help of [Manchester Chief Constable] Sir James [Anderton].'

Harvey Mason has a receipt from 1985 sent to his father to cover travel expenses for an interview. It was signed by Chester Stern of the *Mail on Sunday*. However, no article on the case was published, either in the *Mail* or any other paper.

To be clear, it has not been possible to directly corroborate the Masons' claim that David Solomon and James McCann were doing business together in Anglesey in 1972. On the other hand, the evidence doesn't refute the possibility that they were. The role of Derek Donovan remains murky. His undoubted relationship with Solomon should have been investigated by the police, but there is no evidence that it was.

John Mason, in trying to make sense of his brush with the criminal underworld, was probing an area which the forces of the state felt should be protected from public scrutiny. There are people today on both sides of the 'divide' in Northern Ireland who are campaigning for disclosure of information held by the state regarding their dead or still living relatives whose lives were severely impacted – and sometimes terminated – by events involving the security services. Senior police officers who often liaised with the security services were expected to maintain silence or deny any knowledge of security matters, under penalty of having their careers and pensions curtailed. Many journalists and politicians adhered to the same code of silence. Such was the case in the 1970s; and not much has changed. Britain is still a notoriously secretive society.

In the covert wars on drugs and terrorism, John and Cynthia Mason were civilian casualties: caught up in something not of their making or understanding; asking questions that made police officers uncomfortable; and suffering consequences. John Mason died in 2013. Cynthia died in 2016. In Harvey Mason's words, 'My father died an angry man.'

Bibliography

Stephen Bentley, *Undercover: Operation Julie - The Inside Story* (CreateSpace: 2016).

David Black, *Psychedelic Tricksters; A True Secret History of LSD* (BPC: 2020).

Rory Cormac, *Disrupt and Deny: Spies, Special Forces, and the Secret Pursuit of British Foreign Policy* (Oxford University Press: 2018)

B Cox, J Shirley and M Short, *The Fall of Scotland Yard* (Penguin, London: 1977).

Ronald D Craze, *More Snakes Than Ladders - Book 1* (Independent Publishing Platform: 2013)

Lyn Ebenezer, *Operation Julie: The World's Greatest LSD Bust* (Y Lolfa Cyf: 2010).

Leaf Fielding, *To Live Outside the Law* (Serpent's Tail. London: 2012).

Jonathan Green, *All Dressed Up – The Sixties and the Counter-culture* (Pimlico, London: 1999).

Jonathon Green, *Days in the Life: Voices From the English Underground 1961-71* (Pimlico, London: 2013).

Catherine Hayes and Christine Bott, *The Untold Story of Christine Bott* (Barnham Broom: 2021.

Michael Hollingshead, *The Man Who Turned On the World.* (Blond and Briggs, London: 1973).

Aldous Huxley, *Heaven and Hell* (Chatto and Windus: 1954).

Aldous Huxley, *Texts and Pretexts (1932)*

Adrian Laing, *R.D. Laing A biography* (Adrian Laing: 2012)

Timothy Leary, *Flashbacks: A Personal and Cultural History of an Era* (Heineman:1983).

Martin Lee and Bruce Shlain, *Acid Dreams: The Complete Social History of LSD, the CIA, the Sixties and Beyond* (Grove Press: 1985).

Richard Lee and Colin Pratt, *Operation Julie, How the Undercover Police Team Smashed the World's Greatest Drugs Gang* (WH Allen, London: 1978).

David Leigh, *High Time: the Life and Times of Howard Marks* (Unwin, London 1985.

Howard Marks, *Mr Nice: an Autobiography* (Vintage, London: 1985).

Jonathan Marshall, *The Lebanese Connection: Corruption, Civil War and the International Drug Traffic* (Stanford University Press, 2012).

David May and Stewart Tendler, *The Brotherhood of Eternal Love : From Flower Power to Hippie Mafia - The Story of the LSD* (Panther, London:1984).

Antonio Negri, *Negri on Negri: in conversation with Anne Dufourmentelle* (Routledge, London/New York: 2004).

Martyn Pritchard and Ed Laxton, *Busted! The sensational life-story of an undercover hippie cop* (Daily Mirror Books: 1978).

Charles Radcliffe, *Don't Start Me Talking: Subculture, Situationism and the Sixties* (Bread and Circuses: 2018).

Andy Roberts, *Acid Drops: Adventures in Psychedelia* (Psychedelic Press: 2016).

Andy Roberts, *Albion Dreaming: A popular history of LSD in Britain* (Marshall Cavendish: 2008).

Perry Robinson and Florence Wetzel, *The Traveler* (Writers Club Press: 2002)..

Nick Schou, *Orange Sunshine : the Brotherhood of Eternal Love and its quest to spread peace, love, and acid to the world* (Thomas Dunne Books, New York: 2010)

Herb Snitzer, Glorious *Days and Nights: a Jazz Memoir* (University Press of Mississippi: 2011).

David Solomon, *LSD: The Consciousness-Expanding Drug* (Berkley Publishing Corporation: 1964).

Andrew Tully, *The Secret War Against Dope,* (1973, Kindle Edition, 2015).

Peter Walsh, *Drug War: The Secret History* (Milo Books, London: 2018)

Philip P Willan, *Puppet Masters: The Political Use of Terrorism in Italy* (Universe: 2002).

Articles

Jed Birmingham, 'William Burroughs and David Solomon', RealityStudio: A William S. Burroughs Community.

Modern Literature Collection: 'Transcript of taped conversation between Alexander Trocchi, William S. Burroughs, Ian Dunbar and George Andrews concerning drug addiction'. http://omeka.wustl.edu/omeka/exhibits/show/mlc50/item/9947

Phil Chamberlain, 'The construction industry blacklist: how the Economic League lived on', *Lobster* 58 https://www.lobster-magazine.co.uk/free/lobster58/]

Tim Malyon, 15 Tons and What D'You Get?, *City Limits*, 27 November and 1 December, 1981. Republished by *The Generalist*,https://hqinfo.blogspot.com/2016/04/marks-in-memoriam-howard-making.html

Film

The Sunshine Makers, directed by Cosmo Feilding-Mellen, 2015.

Miscellaneous

All the quotes by Steve Abrams are from an interview conducted by David Black in 1997.

'Voluntary Statement of Richard Hilary Kemp handed to Detective Superintendent Greenslade at Horsfield Prison, Bristol on Friday, 30 December 1977' (unpublished).

Correspondence between David Black and Tim Scully, September 2019 to May 2020.

NAME INDEX

Abrams, Steve. 32-39,62,109,117,118,152

Adams, Charles. 126

Alpert, Richard. 12,21,46

Al-Sadr, Moussa. 123,124

Andrews, George. 64,91,147

Annable, Martin. 75,77,115

Arnaboldi, Paul. 24,26,29,57,59,68,75,76, 78,81,82,95,96,103,106,108,111, 142

Barritt, Brian. 71

Bennerson, Paul. 64-66

Bentley, Stephen. 90,92,98-100, 105, 108, 119, 138-40

Bott, Christine. 9,29,31,56,57,59,71,72,74-78,81,93,94,97,103,105,115-117,119,133-35,138,142

Buda, Franco. 121

Burden, Richard. 77,82,104,115

Burroughs, William. 11,13

Bott, Christine. 9,23.24,28-30,56, 60,70,71,77,89,90,91,95,103, 130-132,136

Bruce. Lenny. 11

Buxton, Alan. 117

Byrne, Johnny. 36

Carson, Rachel. 134

Casa-Grande, Christopher. 116

Condon, Rory. 43

Craze, Ronald. 41,44-48,50-54,85,106

Crewe, Mostyn. 116

Crick, Francis. 33, 34,65

Curcio, Renate. 123

Cuthbertson, Brian. 66,68,74-76,99,101,105-08,115

Dalton, Tony. 77,103,115

Debord, Guy.114

Demarest, Robert. 134

Docherty, Dutch. 154,155

Donovan, Derek. 140-150,161

Donovan, Terry. 146,147

Douglas, Donald. 42

Druce, Michael. 41,43-46,48-54,85,106.138

Ebenezer, Lyn. 84

Evans, Gordon. 116

Fabian, Jenny. 36

Fielding, Leaf. 5,66-69,70, 74,76,77, 102,105-07,116,132

Flannagan, Douglas. 77,100,101,115

Flood, Dougie. 147

Floridia, Giorgio. 125-127

Friedman, Lester. 50,51,54,56

Gaomi, Prof. 17,19,54

Garnet, Bunny. 36

Gillespie, Dizzy. 9,10

Ginsberg, Allen. 11

Godfrey, Derek. 90-92

Goekjian, Sam. 124

Green, Nick. 9,16-19, 20,23-27,111

Greenslade, Dennis. 90,112-114,129,130

Griggs, Carol. 47

Griggs, John. 44,47,106,107

Hansen, Wendy. 126

Harris, Lee, 136

Hauchard, Michel. 70,71

Hayes, Catherine. 135

Healy, Paul. 116

Heasman, John. 116

Hendrix, Jimi, 42

Herbert, George. 89,90

Hesse, Herman. 13

Hitchcock, William 13,41,43,46,51,106

Hoch, Paul. 40

Hofmann, Albert. 74,135

Hollingshead, Michael. 12,20,21

Hoogstraten, Nicholas. 150

Horst, Arend der. 148

Hughes, Alston. 75,77,87,88, 95,98, 99, 100,102,115,116

Hughes, Eurwyn. 81

Hughes, Sheila. 81

Huxley, Aldous. 10-13

Jones, LeRoi. 11

Johnstone, James. 79

Kaimer, Henriette. 30,121

Kamel, Saleh. 159

Kapur, Victor. 23

Kemp, Richard. 4,16-20,22-32,54-61, 64,65,68,69-81,87,90-97,102,103.105,107-116,122,129-32,138,139,142,152

Kenyon, Monica. 116

Kesey, Ken. 41

Lake, PC. 87

Laing, Ronald. 15, 32,34,61-63,91,117,118

Laing, Utta. 62

Laxton, Ed. 143

Lane, Patrick. 157

Leary, Timothy. 12,13,20,21,23,41,62,70,71,81,91,92,95,106,107,116

Leary, Rosemary. 62

Lee, Martin. 48,55,123

Lee, Richard. 56,84-96,102-08,117-122

Leigh, David. 150

Linker, David. 30,57,122

Littlejohn, Keith. 156

Littlejohn, Kenneth. 155,156
Lloyd. Stephen. 149
Lochhead. William. 77,98,116
Mantell, David. 124
Marcuson. Alan. 151-153
Marcuson, Jill. 151
Marks, Howard. 139, 150-56
Mason, Cynthia. 140,144,159
Mason, Harvey. 140,159,161,162
Mason, John. 138-145,149,152-62
Maxwell, Susan, 159-160
May, John. 114,136
McCann, James. 139-140,144,150-59
McCartan, Peter. 150
McDonnell, John. 77,98
McMillan, Hamilton. 154,155
Mechoulem, Prof. 17, 19, 33,54
Mellen, Joey. 20
Mendelsohn, Felix de. 150,151
Metzger, Ralph. 21
Miller, Henry. 11
Munro, Andrew. 25,26,70,74,75,95,101,104-109,115
Munson, Donald. 49
Myers, Philip. 89,159,160
Natham, Harry. 23
Nutt, David. 133,136
Nunziata, Claudio. 125,126
Nuttall, Jeff. 20
O'Brien, Desmond. 20
O'Brien, Patrick. 131
O'Hanlon, Charles. 90,91
Osborne, Christopher. 116

171

Osmond, Humphrey. 13

Owsley, Bear Stanley. 41-46,74

Pakhula, Ruth, 43

Panting, Peter. 94

Park, Justice 116

Parker-Rhodes, Adam. 35

Pelopida, Nicolas. 116

Petroff-Tchomakov, Vladimir. 96

Plinston, Graham. 151

Pountain, Dick. 33,35,69,152,153

Preece, John. 77,115

Pritchard, Martyn. 6,85,86,98,102-117,143

Radcliffe, Charles. 148-151,153,156

Randall, Michael. 44,46,59,83,84,105

Redfearn, John. 87

Rees, Dai. 104

Rees, Hilary. 77,97

Richardson, Charles.145,146,150

Richardson, Eddie. 145

Roberts, Andy. 93,99

Robertson, David. 116

Robinson, Perry. 11,12

Russoniello, Joseph. 127

Sand, Nick. 44-55,74,74,106,124,12755,73,104,122,125

Scully. Tim. 41-50, 74, 106,124, 125,126, 127,128

Sheni, Izchak 'Zahi' (or Zani). 64,77,83, 104,106,108,111,112,119,124,127,128

Shlain, Bruce. 48,55,123

Simons, Bernie. 152

Snitzer, Herb. 10

Solomon, David. 9-18, 22-25,27, 28,31-36, 48,57,59, 64,65,68-83. 90-93,101,104,106.108-112,115,117,122,136-144,150,152,159

Solomon, Kim. 9,16,26,112

Solomon, Lynne.8

Solomon, Pat.9,19,26,71,72

Spear, Bing. 36,85,117

Spenceley, Russell. 77,87,102,115

Spenceley, Janine. 116

Stalker, John. 161

Stark, Ronald. 28-32,34-39,48-63,84,92, 107,119-128,152,153

Stern, Chester, 159

Stevens, Joe. 150,151

Svenson, Tord. 23,48,124

Taylor, Philip. 126

Tcharney, Mark. 75,77,82,97, 105,107, 108,109, 111,112,115,117,118,120

Thomas, Gerald. 69,70,79,80,90,91,92,95, 101,106,112,115,117142,143

Thomas, Richard. 89

Todd, David.115

Todd, Henry. 65-68,74-77,90,101, 102,105, 109,129

Tokhi, Aman and Nasrullah.39

Trocchi, Alexander. 20,64

Walsh, Peter. 95,147,155

Walton, Simon. 29,50,51,57,79,92

Watts, Alan. 13

Webley-Everard, Glynne.36,63

Wooton, Barbara.30

Wright, Eric. 96,100

Printed in Great Britain
by Amazon